CHOOSING THE HYMNS

for use with the Church of Ireland
Alternative Prayer Book 1984

EDWARD DARLING

COLLINS

Collins Liturgical Publications
distributed in Ireland by
Educational Company of Ireland
21 Talbot Street, Dublin 1

Collins Liturgical Publications
187 Piccadilly, London W1V 9DA

ISBN 0 00 599807 7
First published 1984

Printed in Great Britain by
Richard Clay (The Chaucer Press) Ltd,
Bungay, Suffolk

CONTENTS

FOREWORD

by the Archbishop of Armagh
The Most Reverend John W. Armstrong, D.D.

This guide fulfils a great need for the busy parish clergyman and is a very worthy successor to former similar guides. The changing liturgical forms and the issue of a new Lectionary have reduced the usefulness of those older guides. This careful choice of hymns in the present volume for each Sunday of the year, as well as the Saints' Days and other special occasions, is taken both from the Irish Church Hymnal and the other allowed books. Such a choice makes for variety for the congregation and a musical challenge to the choirs. Too often in our churches the hymns chosen for services have been repeated with regularity, but the use of this new guide compiled by Edward Darling makes certain of an interesting and moving worship.

Church Organists and Choir Masters should welcome this guide because its is produced not in an academic way, but by someone who is a practical church musician and a busy parish clergyman.

Therefore it gives me great pleasure to commend this guide to all who have the ordering of church services, both clerical and lay, and congratul-ate the compiler on the excellent format of the guide.

+ JOHN ARMAGH:

Pentecost 1984

PREFACE

When a revised Lectionary for experimental use in the Church of Ireland was introduced in 1973, it became obvious that, sooner or later, a new hymn guide would need to be produced; for, clearly, the suggested selection of hymns for Sundays and Holy Days, which appears at the back of the musical volume of the current edition of the *Irish Church Hymnal*, was chosen to accompany the Lectionary in the Book of Common Prayer. And so, as soon as the two-year cycle of readings came into use, I began to draw up my own personal list of what I felt were suitable hymns for our changing patterns of worship.

The following years saw the publication of a number of useful guides for choosing hymns appropriate to the Series 3 Eucharistic Lectionary, some in individual booklet form and some incorporated into the more contemporary hymnals such as *Hymns for Today's Church* and the new standard edition of *Hymns Ancient and Modern*. Perhaps the most comprehensive of these guides has been the English publication *Hymns with the New Lectionary*. Its compiler, Robin Leaver, has drawn from some twenty-seven different hymnals, in order to produce a list of hymns highlighting the thematic emphasis of the revised Lectionary and with a specific bearing on the particular Psalm, Old Testament reading, Epistle or Gospel, as the case may be.

It was this guide more than any other which prompted and stimulated me to produce a comprehensive selection of hymns as a companion to the main eucharistic readings in the Church of Ireland Alternative Prayer Book 1984.

What is now being offered, therefore, is an index of hymns for the principal Sunday themes, the Saints' Days and Holy Days, and the various special occasions for which psalms and readings have been specially chosen. Its aim has been to select not necessarily the most popular hymns, but rather those which are most appropriate and relevant to the thematic readings. The main eucharistic readings have been printed so that one can see at a glance what is the most suitable hymn for a particular reading. Where no hymn accompanies any one reading - and, sadly, this is all too often the case - it simply means than an *obvious* hymn has not readily come to mind; though this is not to suggest that those who use this hymn guide will not be able to think of a relevant hymn and write it for themselves beside the reading. In any case, there also appears for each day a 'General Choice' of hymns, all of which have some bearing on the theme of the readings, and which should provide clergy and organists alike with a reasonable number of hymns in keeping with the theme of the day.

The hymns which are selected for the specific readings are normally printed in the order that is felt to be the most appropriate or relevant, whereas the hymns selected as the 'General Choice' appear in numerical order. Selections from the Christmas Carols section of the Church Hymnal are shown with a capital C before the number.

RECORDED CHURCH MUSIC

A feature of this particular hymn guide, and one which probably does not appear in any other similar publication, is that certain hymns are marked with an asterisk. This is simply an indication that they are currently available in the Recorded Church Music, which has been such a blessing to the Church of Ireland in recent years, particularly in small country parishes which find it difficult, because of inadequate resources, to provide their own 'live' music. It is to be hoped that with the advent of more sophisticated hi-fi equipment - nowadays easily obtainable and often more cheaply than in the past - a new selection of hymns in keeping with the thematic Lectionary will be made available on cassette tape. However, nothing can replace spontaneous live music, and this should be regarded as the norm for accompanying our services, wherever possible.

THE PSALMS

It should be noted that, as in the Lectionary printed in the Alternative Prayer Book, the verses of the psalms are those of *The Psalms, a new translation for worship (Collins)*. Where such numbers differ from the corresponding verses in the more traditional and familiar Psalter, the Prayer Book versification is printed in brackets.

One might wonder why it is necessary to choose hymns based on the Psalms - particularly those hymns which happen to be straightforward metrical psalms - for, if the Psalm has already been sung or said at a service, why repeat it in another form? It is my belief, however, that the occasion may arise when a more informal type of non-liturgical act of worship will be used on the theme of the day and which will not necessarily include the traditional type of psalm. On such an occasion, the Old Hundredth (Hymn 333: 'All people that on earth do dwell') - to quote just one example - might well prove to be far more fitting and appropriate, especially if the service is of an interdenominational nature, where Christians are present who have never been accustomed to singing psalms set to Anglican chant.

HYMNALS REFERRED TO

The guide includes suggestions of hymns not only from the *Irish Church Hymnal*, but also from *Hymns for Today* - formerly produced in two volumes (each containing a hundred hymns for modern use), entitled *100 Hymns for Today* and *More Hymns for Today*. The House of Bishops has sanctioned this combined hymnal for general use throughout the Church of Ireland, and such authorization should serve to enrich our worship, especially when hymns based on the thematic Lectionary are not readily to be found in the Church Hymnal. These additional hymns are easily distinguishable in the guide from the more traditional ones in our own Hymnal, in that they are marked with a † after the hymn number.

Some twenty-three hymns are common to both hymnals. A list of these is printed on page 191. Whenever a hymn appears in both collections, it is the *Irish Church Hymnal* number which is given, as that is likely to be the more widely used book, The one exception to this rule is 'Hills of the north, rejoice', as the revised version in *Hymns for Today* (no.137), seems more meaningful and relevant in our contempoary understanding of Christian mission.

Some of the duplicated hymns are shorter in one collection than in the other, and only eleven have the same tune in each book. This should allow for flexibility when a shortened form is desired or a good alternative tune required.

Parishes wishing to use *Hymns for Today* in conjunction with the *Irish Church Hymnal* should note that a generous 25% grant is given by the Council of Hymns Ancient and Modern on all new bulk orders. Details as to how to apply for these grants can be obtained from Hymns Ancient and Modern, St.Mary's Works, St. Mary's Plain, Norwich, Norfolk NR3 3BH.

THE LECTIONARY INDEX

The final section of the guide contains an index of all the readings in the Lectionary, from which the hymns (or lack of them!) have been chosen and selected. This could be of particular value to the clergy when they wish to find a hymn based on a passage of scripture from which they might be preaching.

APPRECIATION

Thanks must be expressed to the Very Reverend Brian Mayne (Dean of

Waterford) for his guidance on the Lectionary passages - it was he who was responsible for compiling and, where necessary, modifying the Lectionary that appears in the Alternative Prayer Book - and to Canon Victor Dungan for his helpful advice on the hymns which are available in Recorded Church Music - an area where he was actively involved right from its inception. Appreciation is also recorded of the encouragement and support given to the idea of this hymn guide by the Chairman and members of the Liturgical Advisory Committee.

There are probably many inadequacies and shortcomings in this guide, but it is hoped that all those involved in leading us in worship will find it helpful in selecting the most suitable hymns, whether old or new, that will bring our worship to life, so that what we offer to Almighty God will be a worthy expression of our praise for him.

Edward Darling
May 1984

SECTION 1

HYMNS FOR SUNDAYS, PRINCIPAL HOLY DAYS AND SEASONS

THE NINTH SUNDAY BEFORE CHRISTMAS

Theme : The Creation

YEAR 1

Psalm

104, 1-10   (1-9)

    339   God is a Name my soul adores
* 353   O worship the King all-glorious above

Old Testament

Genesis 1, 1-3 & 24-31a

* 284   Thou whose almighty word
    346   All creatures of our God and King
* 349   I sing the almighty power of God
    351   Lord of beauty, thine the splendour
    356   The spacious firmament on high
    115 †   Come, Holy Ghost, our hearts inspire

Epistle

Colossians 1, 15-20

    105   Nature with open volume stands
* 322   Be thou my vision, O Lord of my heart

Gospel

John 1, 1-14

    270   Christ is the world's true Light
    492   All my hope on God is founded
    135 †   God who spoke in the beginning

YEAR 2

Psalm

29

Old Testament

Genesis 2, 4b-9 & 15-25

* 602   All things bright and beautiful
* 402   Breathe on me, Breath of God

For the Epistle

Revelation 4

* 331   Holy, Holy, Holy! Lord God Almighty
    354   Praise the Lord! ye heavens adore him
* 474   Angel voices, ever singing
    452   God reveals his presence
* 590   Love Divine, all loves excelling

Gospel

John 3, 1-8

    162   Spirit of mercy, truth, and love

General Choice

THE EIGHTH SUNDAY BEFORE CHRISTMAS

Theme : The Fall

YEAR 1

Psalm   130

Old Testament   Genesis 4, 1-10

          104   Glory be to Jesus
          141 † In Adam we have all been one

Epistle   1 John 3, 9-18

          540   O brother man! Fold to thy heart thy brother
          517   Gracious Spirit, Holy Ghost
          518   Help us to help each other, Lord
          568   Jesus, thy Blood and righteousness

Gospel   Mark 7, 14-23

          522   Be thou my guardian and my guide
          606   Do no sinful action

YEAR 2

Psalm   10, 13-20

Old Testament   Genesis 3, 1-15

          36 †   God who created this Eden of earth
         185 †   Walking in a garden
         191 †   What Adam's disobedience cost
         580   Jesu, grant me this, I pray

Epistle   Romans 7, 7-13

     * 359   All hail the power of Jesu's Name

Gospel   John 3, 13-21

     * 330   Father, of heaven, whose love profound
     * 388   Praise to the Holiest in the height
       377   My blessed Saviour, is the love
       270   Christ is the world's true Light

General Choice

	96	Sinful, sighing to be blest
	105	Nature with open volume stands
	112	Sing, my tongue, the glorious battle
	410	Almighty Father, who dost give
	543	O God of truth, whose living word
	561	Lord, when we bend before thy throne
*	570	Just as I am, without one plea
	670	Souls of men, why will ye scatter
	18 †	Creator of the earth and skies
	51 †	Lo, in the wilderness a voice
	92 †	The God who rules this earth
	156 †	Lord God, your love has called us here
	160 †	Lord of the boundless curves of space
	189 †	We turn to you, O God of every nation

THE SEVENTH SUNDAY BEFORE CHRISTMAS

Theme   :   The Election of God's People - Abraham

YEAR 1

Psalm   1

Old Testament   Genesis 12, 1-9

      169 † O raise your eyes on high and see
      332   The God of Abraham praise
    * 506   O God of Bethel, by whose hand

Epistle   Romans 4, 13-25

    * 562   O help us, Lord; each hour of need

Gospel   John 8, 51-59

YEAR 2

Psalm   105, 1-11

Old Testament   Genesis 22, 1-18

      169 † O raise your eyes on high and see
      332   The God of Abraham praise
    * 506   O God of Bethel, by whose hand

Epistle   James 2, 14-24

    * 562   O help us, Lord; each hour of need

Gospel   Luke 20, 9-17

General Choice

THE SIXTH SUNDAY BEFORE CHRISTMAS

Theme   :   The Promise of Redemption - Moses

YEAR 1

Psalm   135, 1-6

Old Testament   Exodus 3, 7-15

                  131   Come, ye faithful, raise the strain
                  155 †   Lord God, we give you thanks for all
                                        your saints

Epistle   Hebrews 3, 1-6

                  358   Awake and sing the song

Gospel   John 6, 25-35

                  217   Bread of heaven, on thee we feed
               * 219   Bread of the world, in mercy broken
                  227   I hunger and I thirst
               * 229   Jesu, thou Joy of loving hearts
               * 236   O God, unseen, yet ever near

YEAR 2

Psalm   77, 11-20

                  497   God moves in a mysterious way

Old Testament   Exodus 6, 2-8

                  445   There is a land of pure delight
               * 485   Through all the changing scenes of life
                  131   Come, ye faithful, raise the strain

Epistle   Hebrews 11, 17-31

Gospel   Mark 13, 5-13

                  521   Believe not those who say
               * 322   Be thou my vision, O Lord of my heart

General Choice

	5	Let the morn be holy
	217	Bread of heaven, on thee we feed
	223	Father, we thank thee who hast planted
	228	Jesus, to thy table led
*	234	Lord, enthroned in heavenly splendour
	320	Alone with none but thee, my God
	492	All my hope on God is founded
*	493	Children of the heavenly King
*	496	Guide me, O thou great Jehovah
*	506	O God of Bethel, by whose hand
	528	Eternal Ruler of the ceaseless round
*	556	Through the night of doubt and sorrow
	574	Come unto me, ye weary

THE FIFTH SUNDAY BEFORE CHRISTMAS

Theme : The Remnant of Israel

YEAR 1

Psalm   80, 1-7

Old Testament   1 Kings 19, 9-18
                             * 575   Dear Lord and Father of mankind

Epistle   Romans 11, 13-24

Gospel   Matthew 24, 37-44
                             432   Thy kingdom come! on bended knee

YEAR 2

Psalm   80, 8-19

Old Testament   Isaiah 10, 20-23
                             * 50   O come, O come, Emmanuel

Epistle   Romans 9, 19-28

Gospel   Mark 13, 14-23
                             * 504   O God, our help in ages past

General Choice

	224	From glory to glory, advancing, we praise thee, O Lord
	279	Lift up your heads, ye gates of brass
*	293	Eternal Father, strong to save
*	411	City of God, how broad and far
	423	Lord of our life, and God of our salvation
*	430	The Church's one foundation
*	431	Thy hand, O God, has guided
	457	Jesus, where'er thy people meet
	473	A safe stronghold our God is still
	484	Sing praise to God who reigns above
*	485	Through all the changing scenes of life .
*	496	Guide me, O thou great Jehovah
	499	Jesus, still lead on
*	501	Lead us, heavenly Father, lead us
	507	Oft in danger, oft in woe
*	556	Through the night of doubt and sorrow
*	575	Dear Lord and Father of mankind
	83 †	Praise the Lord, rise up rejoicing

THE FIRST SUNDAY IN ADVENT
Theme   :   The Advent Hope

YEAR 1

Psalm   50, 1-6

Old Testament   Isaiah 52, 7-10

Epistle   1 Thessalonians 5, 1-11

                46   Hark! 'tis the watchman's cry
              72 † O Day of God, draw nigh

Gospel   Luke 21, 25-33

     * 47   Lo! he comes; with clouds descending
     413   Lift up your heads, ye mighty gates
     420   Hark what a sound, and too divine for hearing

YEAR 2

Psalm   82

Old Testament   Isaiah 51, 4-11

Epistle   Romans 13, 8-14

     * 44   Hark! a thrilling voice is sounding
      9 †   Awake, awake: fling off the night!
   104 †   Away with gloom, away with doubt

Gospel   Matthew 25, 31-46

   100 †   When I needed a neighbour, were you there?
   675   Thou didst leave thy throne and thy kingly crown
   533   Jesu, thou divine Companion

General Choice	* 43	Come, thou long-expected Jesus
	* 45	Hark the glad sound! the Saviour comes
	49	The advent of our King
	* 50	O come, O come, Emmanuel
	218	By Christ redeemed, in Christ restored
	248	'Till he come' - O let the words
	270	Christ is the world's true Light
	279	Lift up your heads, ye gates of brass
	374	Jesus came, the heavens adoring
	375	Lord of mercy and of might
	* 391	Ten thousand times ten thousand
	394	Thou art coming, O my Saviour
	413	Lift up your heads, ye mighty gates
	418	Hail to the Lord's Anointed
	* 421	Jesus shall reign where'er the sun
	424	Mine eyes have seen the glory of the coming of the Lord
	* 429	Thy kingdom come, O God
	432	Thy kingdom come! on bended knee
	* 548	Soldiers of Christ, arise
	686	Sleepers wake! for night is flying
	64 †	Lord, save thy world; in bitter need
	137 †	Hills of the North, rejoice

THE SECOND SUNDAY IN ADVENT

Theme : The Word of God in the Old Testament

YEAR 1

Psalm   19, 7-14   (7-15)

Old Testament   Isaiah 55, 1-11

Epistle   2 Timothy 3, 14- 4,5

         282   Spread, O spread, thou mighty word
         158 †   Lord Jesus Christ, be present now

Gospel   John 5, 36 -47

       * 470   Lord, thy word abideth

YEAR 2

Psalm   119, 129-136

Old Testament   Isaiah 64, 1-7

         457 .   Jesus, where'er thy people meet

Epistle   Romans 15, 4-13

         134 †   God, who has caused to be written thy
                  word for our learning
         135 †   God who spoke in the beginning
         468   God hath spoken - by his prophets
         538   Lord, be thy word my rule
         195 †   Where love and loving-kindness dwell
         192 †   When Christ was lifted from the earth

Gospel   Luke 4, 14-21

       * 45   Hark the glad sound! the Saviour comes
        467   Father of mercies, in thy word

General Choice

48	O heavenly Word, eternal Light
218	By Christ redeemed, in Christ restored
248	'Till he come' - O let the words
* 284	Thou whose almighty word
404	Holy Spirit, hear us
* 421	Jesus shall reign where'er the sun
469	How precious is the Book divine
* 471	Word of the living God
472	O Word of God incarnate
* 612	I love to hear the story
* 620	Jesus loves me: this I know
673	Tell me the old, old story
40 †	Help us, O Lord, to learn
68 †	Not far beyond the sea, nor high
72 †	O Day of God draw nigh
86 †	Sing we a song of high revolt
90 †	Thanks to God whose Word was spoken
113 †	Christians, lift up your hearts, and make this a day of rejoicing
115 †	Come, Holy Ghost, our hearts inspire
157 †	Lord, I have made thy word my choice
176 †	Rise and hear! The Lord is speaking
180 †	The prophets spoke in days of old

THE THIRD SUNDAY IN ADVENT

Theme   :   The Forerunner

YEAR 1

Psalm	126	
Old Testament	Isaiah 40, 1-11	
	51 †	Lo, in the wilderness a voice
	* 51	On Jordan's bank the Baptist's cry
Epistle	1 Corinthians 4, 1-5	
	551	Son of God, eternal Saviour
	257	O Thou who makest souls to shine
	258	Pour out thy Spirit from on high
Gospel	John 1, 19-28	
	175	The great forerunner of the morn
	* 45	Hark the glad sound! the Saviour comes
	* 50	O come, O come, Emmanuel
	51 †	Lo, in the wilderness a voice

YEAR 2

Psalm	Benedictus	
Old Testament	Malachi 3, 1-5	
	* 3	Christ, whose glory fills the skies
	46	Hark! 'tis the watchman's cry
Epistle	Philippians 4, 4-9	
	397	Rejoice, the Lord is King!
	476	Fill thou my life, O Lord my God
	567	There is no sorrow, Lord, too light
	* 679	What a friend we have in Jesus
Gospel	Matthew 11, 2-15	
	* 51	On Jordan's bank the Baptist's cry
	175	The great forerunner of the morn
	* 382	O for a thousand tongues to sing
	66 †	Lord, we are blind; the world of sight

24

General Choice

*	44	Hark! a thrilling voice is sounding
*	47	Lo! he comes; with clouds descending
	49	The advent of our King
	218	By Christ redeemed, in Christ restored
	248	'Till he come' - O let the words
	257	O Thou who makest souls to shine
	258	Pour out thy Spirit from on high
	269	Lord, speak to me, that I may speak
	270	Christ is the world's true Light
	557	Ye servants of the Lord
*	590	Love Divine, all loves excelling
	9 †	Awake, awake: fling off the night!
	40 †	Help us, O Lord, to learn

THE FOURTH SUNDAY IN ADVENT

Theme   :   The Annunciation

YEAR 1

Psalm   45, 10-17   (11-18)

Old Testament   Isaiah 11, 1-9

	C12	I know a rose-tree springing
	274	God is working his purpose out as year succeeds to year
*	50	O come, O come, Emmanuel

Epistle   1 Corinthians 1, 26-31

	420	Hark what a sound, and too divine for hearing
	413	Lift up your heads, ye mighty gates

Gospel   Luke 1, 26-38a

	172	Praise we the Lord this day
	151 †	Long ago, prophets knew
	27 †	For Mary, Mother of our Lord
*	43	Come, thou long-expected Jesus

YEAR 2

Psalm   Magnificat

	89 †	Tell out, my soul, the greatness of the Lord
	86 †	Sing we a song of high revolt

Old Testament   Zechariah 2, 10-13

	286	Zion's King shall reign victorious

For the Epistle   Revelation 21, 1-7

	76 †	O Holy City, seen of John
	441	O what the joy and the glory must be
*	439	Light's abode, celestial Salem
	343	Songs of praise the angels sang
*	590	Love Divine, all loves excelling

Gospel   Matthew I, 18-23

         *   C4   As Joseph was a-walking
            67   Of the Father's love begotten
          399   To the Name of our salvation
        * 596   How sweet the Name of Jesus sounds

General Choice

            45   Hark the glad sound! The Saviour comes
            58   From east to west, from shore to shore
          343   Songs of praise the angels sang
          432   Thy kingdom come! on bended knee
        * 437   Jerusalem the golden
           C3   A virgin most pure, as the prophets foretold
        199 †   Ye watchers and ye holy ones

The readings appointed for Christmas Eve take precedence over the readings of the weekdays following the Fourth Sunday in Advent. If, however, Christmas Day falls on a Monday, the Sunday readings are those set out above. No guide, therefore, is given as to a choice of hymns suitable for use on Christmas Eve.

In parishes where there is a midnight Eucharist on Christmas Eve, the hymns suggested for Christmas Day should be used.

CHRISTMAS DAY

Theme : The Birth of Christ

Psalm   85

96

   * 466   Worship the Lord in the beauty
                         of holiness

98

   165 † New songs of celebration render

Old Testament   Isaiah 9, 2-7

    81   The people that in darkness sat
    C26   Unto us is born a Son

Isaiah 62, 10-12

Micah 5, 2-4

    66   O little town of Bethlehem

Epistle   Titus 2, 11-14 & 3, 3-7

  * 61   Hark! the herald-angels sing

1 John 4, 7-14

   515   Beloved, let us love: love is of God
   341   God is love: let heaven adore him
   31 † God is Light

Hebrews 1, 1-5

  * 64   O come all ye faithful
   67   Of the Father's love begotten
  * 61   Hark! the herald-angels sing

Gospel   Luke 2, 1-14

Luke 2, 8-20

   57   Christians, awake, salute the happy morn
  * 68   While shepherds watched their flocks by nig

C9	God rest you merry, gentlemen
C17	See amid the winter's snow
* C29	When the crimson sun had set
* 624	Once in royal David's city
C2	A child this day is born
55	Blessed night, when first that plain
60	Love came down at Christmas
59	From heaven high I come to you
* 585	Jesus, good above all other
682	Break forth, O beauteous heav'nly light

John 1, 1-14

* 64	O come, all ye faithful
52	A great and mighty wonder
135 †	God who spoke in the beginning
31 †	God is Light

General Choice

399	To the Name of our salvation
551	Son of God, eternal Saviour
67 †	No use knocking on the window
129 †	'Glory to God!' all heav'n with joy is ringing

THE SUNDAY AFTER CHRISTMAS DAY

Themes : The Incarnation (Year 1)
The Presentation (Year 2)

YEAR 1

Psalm	2	
	* 429	Thy kingdom come, O God
Old Testament	Isaiah 7, 10-14	
	56	Child in the manger
Epistle	Galatians 4, 1-7	
	491	Behold the amazing gift of love
Gospel	John 1, 14-18	
	* 64	O come, all ye faithful
	52	A great and mighty wonder
	67	Of the Father's love begotten
	135 †	God who spoke in the beginning
	468	God hath spoken - by his prophets
General Choice	52	A great and mighty wonder
	* 53	Angels from the realms of glory
	551	Son of God, eternal Saviour
	44 †	In humble gratitude, O God
	58 †	Lord Jesus Christ
	65 †	Lord that descendedst, Holy Child
	129 †	'Glory to God!' all heav'n with joy is ringing
	137 †	Hills of the North, rejoice
	151 †	Long ago, prophets knew
	178 †	The great Creator of the worlds
	194 †	Where is this stupendous stranger?

YEAR 2

Psalm	116. 11-18 (11-16)
Old Testament	1 Samuel 1, 20-28
Epistle	Romans 12, 1-8

         * 669   Take my life, and let it be
         * 466   Worship the Lord in the beauty of holiness

Gospel   Luke 2, 22-40

          169   In his temple now behold him
         * 590   Love Divine, all loves excelling
         120 †   Faithful vigil ended

General Choice

            4   Forth in thy Name, O Lord, I go
       * 53   Angels, from the realms of glory
         58   From east to west, from shore to shore
         60   Love came down at Christmas
       476   Fill thou my life, O Lord my God
     * 523   Blest are the pure in heart
       664   My God, accept my heart this day
       681   How brightly beams the morning star!
       684   O Jesu so meek, O Jesu so kind
     131 †   God is here; as we his people
     166 †   Now from the altar of our hearts

THE SECOND SUNDAY AFTER CHRISTMAS

Themes : 'My Father's House'   (Year 1)
              The Light of the World   (Year 2)

YEAR 1

Psalm

Psalm 27, 1-8   (1-7)

Old Testament

Ecclesiasticus 3, 2-7

Exodus 12, 21-27

Epistle

Romans 8, 11-17

* 405   Come, gracious Spirit, heavenly Dove
  528   Eternal Ruler of the ceaseless round
   26 †   Filled with the Spirit's power, with one accord

Gospel

Luke 2, 41-52

   80   The heavenly Child in stature grows
* 612   I love to hear the story
  619   Jesus, Friend of little children

General Choice

  291   Our Father, by whose Name
  413   Lift up your heads, ye mighty gates
* 624   Once in royal David's city
   61 †   Lord of all hopefulness, Lord of all joy
   74 †   O God in heaven, whose loving plan
  140 †   I come with joy to meet my Lord
  149 †   Life is great† So sing about it

Psalm	67	
	* 417	God of mercy, God of grace
Old Testament	Isaiah 60, 1-6	
	418	Hail to the Lord's Anointed
For the Epistle	Revelation 21, 22-22, 5	
	* 415	Glorious things of thee are spoken
	* 437	Jerusalem the golden
	* 439	Light's abode, celestial Salem
Gospel	Matthew 2, 1-12 & 19-23	
	* 77	As with gladness men of old
	* 78	Earth has many a noble city
	* 79	Brightest and best of the sons of the morning
	* C23	The first Nowell the angel did say
	* C26	Unto us is born a Son
General Choice	81	The people that in darkness sat
	270	Christ is the world's true Light
	* 284	Thou whose almighty word
	362	Come, let us join our cheerful songs
	* 466	Worship the Lord in the beauty of holiness
	* 534	Just as I am, thine own to be
	* 624	Once in royal David's city
	9 †	Awake, awake: fling off the night!
	66 †	Lord, we are blind ; the world of sight
	105 †	Can man by searching find out God

Psalm   72, 1-8   *or*   72, 10-21   (10-19)

      418   Hail to the Lord's Anointed
* 421   Jesus shall reign where'er the sun

Old Testament   Isaiah 49, 1-6

Epistle   Ephesians 3, 1-12

    277   In Christ there is no east or west
    278   Light of them that sit in darkness!

Gospel   Matthew 2, 1-12

*   77   As with gladness men of old
*   78   Earth has many a noble city
*   79   Brightest and best of the sons of the morning
*   C23   The first Nowell the angel did say
*   632   The wise may bring their learning
   129 †   'Glory to God!' all heav'n with joy is ringing
   C30   Ye shepherds, leave your flocks upon the mountains
   C27   We three kings of Orient are

General Choice

*	3	Christ, whose glory fills the skies
	18	Hail, gladdening Light, of his pure glory poured
*	19	Holy Father, cheer our way
*	53	Angels, from the realms of glory
	81	The people that in darkness sat
	105	Nature with open volume stands
	270	Christ is the world's true Light
	271	Fling out the banner! let it float
	280	Let the song go round the earth
	282	Spread, O spread, thou mighty word
*	284	Thou whose almighty word
	336	Eternal God, whose power upholds
*	359	All hail the power of Jesu's Name
*	373	In the Name of Jesus
	385	O Love, how deep, how broad, how high!
*	411	City of God, how broad and far
*	415	Glorious things of thee are spoken
	416	God of Eternity, Lord of the ages
*	417	God of mercy, God of grace
*	466	Worship the Lord in the beauty of holiness
*	585	Jesus, good above all other
	681	How brightly beams the morning star†
	C28	What child is this, who, laid to rest

THE FIRST SUNDAY AFTER THE EPIPHANY

Theme : The Baptism of Jesus

YEAR 1

Psalm   36, 5-10

Old Testament   1 Samuel 16, 1-13a

For the Epistle   Acts 10, 34-38a

       409 O Spirit of the living God

Gospel   Matthew 3, 13-17

       385 O Love, how deep, how broad, how high! (vv.1-3 & 7)
       461 Spirit divine, attend our prayer
       193 † When Jesus Came to Jordan
       109 † Christ, when for us you were baptized

YEAR 2

Psalm   89, 19-30 (20-30)

Old Testament   Isaiah 42, 1-7

Epistle   Ephesians 2, 1-10

       656 Come, thou fount of every blessing
     * 373 In the Name of Jesus (vv.1-5)
       377 My blessed Saviour is thy love

Gospel   John 1, 29-34

       409 O Spirit of the living God
       385 O Love, how deep, how broad, how high! (vv.1-3 & 7)

General Choice

THE SECOND SUNDAY AFTER THE EPIPHANY

Theme : The First Disciples

YEAR 1

Psalm   100

      * 333   All people that on earth do dwell
        334   Before Jehovah's aweful throne

Old Testament   Jeremiah 1, 4-10

For the Epistle   Acts 26, 1 & 9-20

        168   We sing the glorious conquest

Gospel   Mark 1, 14-20

      * 166   Jesus calls us! o'er the tumult
      * 575   Dear Lord and Father of mankind
        283   O Master! when thou callest
          4   Forth, in thy Name, O Lord, I go

YEAR 2

Psalm   145, 1-12

        346   All creatures of our God and King
      * 482   Praise to the Lord, the Almighty,
                   the King of creation

Old Testament   1 Samuel 3, 1-10

        650   Speak, Lord, in the stillness

Epistle   Galatians 1, 11-24

        270   Christ is the world's true Light

Gospel   John 1, 35-51

      * 166   Jesus calls us! o'er the tumult
      * 575   Dear Lord and Father of mankind
        180   King of saints, to whom the number
       49 †   Jesus our Lord, our King and our God
     102 †   As Jacob with travel was weary one day

General Choice

	197	Disposer supreme, and Judge of the earth
	198	The eternal gifts of Christ the King
	457	Jesus, where'er thy people meet
*	501	Lead us, heavenly Father, lead us
*	534	Just as I am, thine own to be
*	544	O Jesus, I have promised
*	554	Take up thy cross, the Saviour said
	563	O Thou who camest from above
*	585	Jesus, good above all other
	656	Come, thou fount of every blessing
	664	My God, accept my heart this day
*	669	Take my life, and let it be
	49 †	Jesus our Lord, our King and our God
	59 †	Lord Jesus, once you spoke to men
	152 †	Lord, as I wake I turn to you
	186 †	We are your people
	196 †	Who are we who stand and sing?

THE THIRD SUNDAY AFTER THE EPIPHANY

Theme : Signs of Glory

YEAR 1

Psalm   46

                         473   A safe stronghold our God is still

Old Testament   Exodus 33, 12-23

                         * 569   Rock of ages, cleft for me

Epistle   1 John 1, 1-7

                         31 †   God is Light
                         472   O Word of God incarnate
                         * 284   Thou whose almighty word

Gospel   John 2, 1-11

                         591   My spirit longs for thee
                         * 453   Jesu, stand among us

YEAR 2

Psalm   107, 1-9

Old Testament   Deuteronomy 8, 1-6

Epistle   Philippians 4, 10-20

                         * 553   Thine for ever! God of love

Gospel   John 6, 1-14

                         227   I hunger and I thirst
                         * 219   Bread of the world, in mercy broken
                         * 496   Guide me, O thou great Jehovah
                         * 506   O God of Bethel, by whose hand

General Choice

THE FOURTH SUNDAY AFTER THE EPIPHAN

Theme : The New Temple

YEAR 1

Psalm   48, 9-13   (8-13)

Old Testament   1 Kings 8, 22-30

Epistle   1 Corinthians 3, 10-17

*	211	Come, ever-blessed Spirit, come
*	430	The Church's one foundation
	449	Christ is our corner-stone

Gospel   John 2, 13-22

	457	Jesus, where'er thy people meet
*	439	Light's abode, celestial Salem
*	465	We love the place, O God

YEAR 2

Psalm   84, 1-7

	456	How lovely are thy dwellings fair
	459	Pleasant are thy courts above

Old Testament   Jeremiah 7, 1-11

Epistle   Hebrews 12, 18-29

*	415	Glorious things of thee are spoken
	434	Jerusalem, my happy home
*	513	To Zion's hill I lift my eyes

Gospel   John 4, 19-26

	162	Spirit of mercy, truth, and love
*	460	Saviour, send a blessing to us
*	369	Hail, thou once despised Jesus!

General Choice	259	Christ is made the sure foundation
	400	When morning gilds the skies
	401	Where high the heavenly temple stands
*	430	The Church's one foundation
	449	Christ is our corner-stone
	454	Lo, God is here : let us adore
*	465	We love the place, O God
*	482	Praise to the Lord, the Almighty, the King of creation
	492	All my hope on God is founded
*	590	Love Divine, all loves excelling
	38 †	Good is our God who made this place
	112 †	Christians, lift up your hearts, and make this a day of rejoicing

THE FIFTH SUNDAY AFTER THE EPIPHANY

Theme   :   The Wisdom of God

YEARS 1 & 2

Psalm

36

     * 344   Immortal, invisible, God only wise

49, 1-12

Old Testament

Proverbs 2, 1-9

     136 †   God, you have giv' n us power to sound

Ecclesiasticus 42, 15-25

     * 349   I sing the almighty power of God
      492   All my hope on God is founded

Epistle

1 Corinthians 3, 18-23

     * 322   Be thou my vision, O Lord of my heart

Gospel

Matthew 12, 38-42

     * 388   Praise to the Holiest in the height

General Choice

Theme   :   Parables

YEARS 1 & 2

Psalm   43

                             25, 1-10   (1-9)

Old Testament   2 Samuel 12, 1-10

Epistle   Romans 1, 18-25

Gospel   Matthew 13, 24-30

                             419   Happy are they, they that love God
                             306   The sower went forth sowing

General Choice

THE NINTH SUNDAY BEFORE EASTER

(SEPTUAGESIMA)

Theme : Christ the Teacher

YEAR 1

Psalm

103, 1-13

    * 481   Praise, my soul, the King of heaven
    * 482   Praise to the Lord, the Almighty, the King of creation

Old Testament

Isaiah 30, 18-21

Epistle

1 Corinthians 4, 8-13

    * 530   Fight the good fight with all thy might!

Gospel

Matthew 5, 1-12

    * 523   Blest are the pure in heart

YEAR 2

Psalm

34, 11-18

    * 485   Through all the changing scenes of life

Old Testament

Proverbs 3, 1-8

    547   Put thou thy trust in God
    600   Lord and Saviour, true and kind

Epistle

1 Corinthians 2, 1-10

Gospel

Luke 8, 4-15

    447   Almighty God, thy word is cast
    176 †   Rise and hear! The Lord is speaking
    306   The sower went forth sowing

General Choice

	196	Captains of the saintly band
	256	Lord of the Church, we humbly pray
	269	Lord, speak to me, that I may speak
	375	Lord of mercy and of might
*	388	Praise to the Holiest in the height
	395	Thou art the Way: to thee alone
	467	Father of mercies, in thy word
*	470	Lord, thy word abideth
*	485	Through all the changing scenes of life
*	498	He who would valiant be
	551	Son of God, eternal Saviour
	555	Teach me, my God and King
	560	Lord, teach us how to pray aright
	599	For Christ to learn, for Christ to teach
*	612	I love to hear the story
	619	Jesus, Friend of little children
	673	Tell me the old, old story
	40 †	Help us, O Lord, to learn
	58 †	Lord Jesus Christ
	59 †	Lord Jesus, once you spoke to me
	84 †	Praise we now the word of grace
	105 †	Can man by searching find out God
	143 †	Jesus, my Lord, let me be near you
	157 †	Lord, I have made thy word my choice
	179 †	'The kingdom is upon you!'
	180 †	The prophets spoke in days of old

49

THE EIGHTH SUNDAY BEFORE EASTER
(SEXAGESIMA)

Theme　:　Christ the Healer

YEAR 1

Psalm　　　　147, 1-11

　　　　　　97　When wounded sore the stricken soul

Old Testament　Zephaniah 3, 14-20

Epistle　　　James 5, 13-16a

　　　*　455　Great Shepherd of thy people, hear
　　　　457　Jesus, where'er thy people meet

Gospel　　　Mark 2, 1-12

　　　　289　Thine arm, O Lord in days of old
　　　　287　From thee all skill and science flow

YEAR 2

Psalm　　　　131

Old Testament　2 Kings 5, 1-14

Epistle　　　2 Corinthians 12, 1-10

　　　*　596　How sweet the Name of Jesus sounds
　　　　361　Conquering kings their titles take

Gospel　　　Mark 7, 24-37

　　　　20　At even, when the sun did set
　　　　371　Immortal love for ever full
　　　*　455　Great Shepherd of thy people, hear

General Choice

THE SEVENTH SUNDAY BEFORE EASTER

(QUINQUAGESIMA)

Theme   :   Christ the Friend of Sinners

YEAR 1

Psalm	32
Old Testament	Hosea 14, 1-7
Epistle	Philemon, 1-16
Gospel	Mark 2, 13-17

	181	He sat to watch o'er customs paid
*	575	Dear Lord and Father of mankind
*	87	Approach, my soul, the mercy seat
*	166	Jesus calls us! o'er the tumult
	50 †	Jesus, whose all-redeeming love
	49 †	Jesus our Lord, our King and our God

YEAR 2

Psalm	119, 65-72
Old Testament	Numbers 15, 32-36
	Isaiah 57, 15-21
Epistle	Colossians 1, 18-23

360	Brethren, let us join to bless
105	Nature with open volume stands

Gospel	John 8, 2-11

667	One there is above all others
541	O for a heart to praise my God

General Choice

	86	All ye who seek for sure relief
	97	When wounded sore the stricken soul
*	109	O sacred head, surrounded
*	214	And now, O Father, mindful of the love
*	322	Be thou my vision, O Lord of my heart
	341	God is love: let heaven adore him
	361	Conquering kings their titles take
*	370	Hallelujah! Sing to Jesus
	377	My blessed Saviour, is thy love
	381	My song is love unknown
	386	O Love, who formedst me to wear
	551	Son of God, eternal Saviour
	568	Jesus, thy Blood and righteousness
*	570	Just as I am, without one plea
	573	As pants the hart for cooling streams
	574	Come unto me, ye weary
*	577	Hark, my soul! it is the Lord
*	579	I heard the voice of Jesus say
*	582	Jesu, lover of my soul
*	585	Jesus, good above all other
*	596	How sweet the Name of Jesus sounds
	648	O for a closer walk with God
	657	Come, ye sinners, poor and wretched
	675	Thou didst leave thy throne and thy kingly crown
*	679	What a Friend we have in Jesus
	29 †	Forgive our sins as we forgive
	50 †	Jesus, whose all-redeeming love
	140 †	I come with joy to meet my Lord
	144 †	Jesus, we thus obey
	156 †	Lord God, your love has called us here
	159 †	Lord of all, to whom alone
	181 †	There in God's garden stands the tree of wisdom
	192 †	When Christ was lifted from the earth
	197 †	With joy we meditate the grace

53

Psalm

6

51, 1-17

90, 1-12

* 504   O God, our help in ages past

Old Testament

Isaiah 58, 1-8

604   As now thy lowly children kneel

Joel 2, 12-17

Amos 5, 6-15

Epistle

1 Corinthians 9,   24-27

* 530   Fight the good fight with all thy might!
520   Awake our souls!   away our fears!

James 4, 1-10

* 552   Stand up, stand up for Jesus

Gospel

Matthew 6, 16-21

92   Lord, who throughout these forty days

Luke 18, 9-14

96   Sinful, sighing to be blest
* 91   Lord Jesu, think on me
561   Lord, when we bend before thy throne
105 †   Can man by searching find out God

General Choice

Any of the Hymns in the Lent section (84 - 98)
or any of the following :-

18 †   Creator of the earth and skies
22(ii)† Father all-loving, thou rulest in majesty
35 †   God of love and truth and beauty
51 †   Lo, in the wilderness a voice
54 †   Lord Christ, when first thou cam'st to men
156 †   Lord God, your love has called us here
159 †   Lord of all, to whom alone

THE FIRST SUNDAY IN LENT

Theme : The King and the Kingdom - Temptation

YEAR 1

Psalm   119, 1-8

Old Testament   Genesis 2, 7-9 & 3, 1-7

      36 † God who created this Eden of earth
     185 † Walking in a garden
     191 † What Adam's disobedience cost
     580   Jesu, grant me this, I pray

Epistle   Hebrews 2, 14-18

  * 501   Lead us, heavenly Father, lead us
    522   Be thou my guardian and my guide
    580   Jesu, grant me this, I pray

Gospel   Matthew 4, 1-11

  * 88   Forty days and forty nights
    92   Lord, who throughout these forty days
   385   O Love, how deep, how broad, how high
           (vv. 1-4 & 7)

YEAR 2

Psalm   91, 1-12

Old Testament   Genesis 4, 1-10

  * 104   Glory be to Jesus
   141 † In Adam we have all been one

Epistle   Hebrews 4, 12-16

   401   Where high the heavenly temple stands
  * 330   Father, of heaven, whose love profound
  197 † With joy we meditate the grace

Gospel	Luke 4, 1-13	
	* 88	Forty days amd forty nights
	92	Lord, who throughout these forty days
	385	O Love, how deep, how broad, how high (vv. 1-4 & 7)
	* 501	Lead us, heavenly Father, lead us
General Choice	20	At even, when the sun did set
	* 87	Approach, my soul, the mercy seat
	91	Lord Jesu, think on me
	380	My God, I love thee; not because
	* 398	We sing the praise of him who died
	423	Lord of our life, and God of our salvation
	473	A safe stronghold our God is still
	507	Oft in danger, oft in woe
	520	Awake our souls! away our fears!
	521	Believe not those who say
	526	Christian, seek not yet repose
	529	Father, who on man dost shower
	* 544	O Jesus, I have promised
	565	Shepherd divine, our wants relieve
	* 569	Rock of ages, cleft for me
	* 575	Dear Lord and Father of mankind
	659	I need thee every hour
	678	Yield not to temptation, for yielding is sin
	54 †	Lord Christ, when first thou cam'st to men

THE SECOND SUNDAY IN LENT

Theme   :   The King and the Kingdom - Conflict

YEAR 1

Psalm	119, 33-40
Old Testament	Genesis 6, 11-22
Epistle	1 John 4, 1-6
	473 A safe stronghold our God is still
Gospel	Luke 19, 41-48
	317 To thee our God we fly (vv. 1-2 & 7-9)
	551 Son of God, eternal Saviour
	492 All my hope on God is founded

YEAR 2

Psalm	18, 18-26 (17-25)
Old Testament	Genesis 7, 17-24
Epistle	1 John 3, 1-10
	491 Behold the amazing gift of love
	385 O Love, how deep, how broad, how high
	(omitting v.6)
Gospel	Matthew 12, 22-32
	638 We have a King who came to earth
	66 † Lord, we are blind; the world of sight

General Choice

THE THIRD SUNDAY IN LENT

Theme : The King and the Kingdom - Suffering

YEAR 1

Psalm 119, 97-104

467   Father of mercies, in thy word

Old Testament Genesis 22, 1-13

*   7   New every morning is the love

Epistle Colossians 1, 24-29

324   How great the tale that there should be

Gospel Luke 9, 18-27

176   Thou art the Christ, O Lord
* 554   Take up thy cross, the Saviour said
49 †   Jesus our Lord, our King and our God
614   It is a thing most wonderful

YEAR 2

Psalm 115, 1-7   (1-8)

Old Testament Genesis 12, 1-9

332   The God of Abraham praise
* 506   O God of Bethel, by whose hand

Epistle 1 Peter 2, 19-25

537   Lord, as to thy dear Cross we flee
505   O happy band of pilgrims

Gospel Matthew 16, 13-28

176   Thou art the Christ, O Lord
* 554   Take up thy cross, the Saviour said
49 †   Jesus our Lord, our King and our God

General Choice

4	Forth, in thy Name, O Lord, I go
74	Father, let me dedicate
102	Alone thou goest forth, O Lord
194	How bright those glorious spirits shine
195	The Son of God goes forth to war
* 369	Hail, thou once-despised Jesus!
380	My God, I love the; not because
* 384	The head that once was crowned with thorns
* 388	Praise to the Holiest in the height
396	Thy life was given for me
* 485	Through all the changing scenes of life
505	O happy band of pilgrims
518	Help us to help each other, Lord
541	O for a heart to praise my God
* 554	Take up thy cross, the Saviour said
* 569	Rock of ages, cleft for me
5 71	When our heads are bowed with woe
572	Art thou weary, heavy-laden
594	O Love that wilt not let me go
670	Souls of men, why will ye scatter
1 †	A Man there lived in Galilee
48 †	Jesus, my Lord, how rich thy grace
55 †	Lord Christ, who on thy heart didst bear
154 †	Lord Christ, we praise your sacrifice

THE FOURTH SUNDAY IN LENT
(commonly called   MOTHERING SUNDAY)

Theme   :   The King and the Kingdom - Transfiguration

YEAR 1

Psalm   119, 153-160

Old Testament   Exodus 34, 29-35

Epistle   2 Corinthians 3, 4-18

      * 453   Jesu, stand among us
      * 590   Love Divine, all loves excelling

Gospel   Luke 9, 28-36

      179   'Tis good, Lord, to be here
      178   Upon the holy Mount they stood
      108 † Christ upon the mountain peak

YEAR 2

Psalm   18, 27-38   (26-37)

Old Testament   Exodus 3, 1-6

      452   God reveals his presence
      155 † Lord God, we give you thanks for all your saint

Epistle   2 Peter 1, 16-19

      * 384   The head that once was crowned with thorns
      536   Light of the lonely pilgrim's heart

Gospel   Matthew 17, 1-13

      179   'Tis good, Lord, to be here
      178   Upon the holy Mount they stood
      169 † O raise your eyes on high and see

General Choice

*	3	Christ, whose glory fills the skies
	224	From glory to glory advancing, we praise Thee, O Lord
	247	Thee we adore, O hidden Saviour, thee
	270	Christ is the world's true Light
*	322	Be thou my vision, O Lord of my heart
*	335	My God, how wonderful thou art
*	369	Hail, thou once-despised Jesus!
	377	My blessed Saviour, is thy love
*	429	Thy kingdom come, O God
	435	Brief life is here our portion
*	437	Jerusalem the golden
*	439	Light's abode, celestial Salem
*	486	When all thy mercies, O my God
	503	O everlasting light
*	523	Blest are the pure in heart
	557	Ye servants of the Lord
	565	Shepherd divine, our wants relieve
	573	As pants the hart for cooling streams
	586	Jesus, these eyes have never seen
	597 (2)	O Jesu, King most wonderful
*	618	Jesus bids us shine with a pure, clear light
	634	Two little eyes to look to God
	644	Let me be with thee, where thou art
	52 †	Lord, as we rise to leave the shell of worship
	59 †	Lord Jesus, once you spoke to men
	200 †	You, living Christ, our eyes behold

Hymns for special Mothering Sunday services
are to be found on pages 175 & 176

63

THE FIFTH SUNDAY IN LENT
(PASSION SUNDAY)

Theme   :   The King and the Kingdom
Victory

YEAR 1

Psalm   76, 1-9

Old Testament   Exodus 6, 2-13

Epistle   Colossians 2, 8-15

                 * 398   We sing the praise of him who died
                   379   Now to him who loved us, gave us

Gospel   John 12, 20-32

                  102   Alone thou goest forth, O Lord
                    13   As now the sun's declining rays

YEAR 2

Psalm   22, 23-29   (22-28)

Old Testament   Jeremiah 31, 31-34

                  541   O for a heart to praise my God

Epistle   Hebrews 9, 11-14

                  222   Draw nigh and take the Body of the Lord
                * 242   Once, only once, and once for all

Gospel   Mark 10, 32-45

                * 116   The royal banners forward go
                112   Sing, my tongue, the glorious battle

General Choice

THE SIXTH SUNDAY IN LENT
(PALM SUNDAY)

Theme   :   The Way of the Cross

Psalm

22, 1-11

24

*	279	Lift up your heads, ye gates of brass
	413	Lift up your heads, ye mighty gates
*	153	See the Conqueror mounts in triumph
*	154	The golden gates are lifted up
	149	Golden harps are sounding
*	150	Hail the day that sees him rise

69, 1-9

45, 1-7 (1-8)

Old Testament

Isaiah 50, 4-9a

Zechariah 9, 9-12

49	The advent of our King

Epistle

Philippians 2, 5-11

*	373	In the Name of Jesus
	4 †	All praise to thee, for thou, O King divi
	614	It is a thing most wonderful
	378	Look, ye saints, the sight is glorious
	598	There is a Name I love to hear

1 Corinthians 1, 18-25

	105	Nature with open volume stands
*	115	When I survey the wondrous Cross
*	398	We sing the praise of him who died
*	113	Sweet the moments, rich in blessing

Gospel		Mark 14, 32- 15, 41 (*or* 15, 1-41)
	117	When my love to Christ grows weak
	526	Christian, seek not yet repose
	381	My song is love unknown (omitting v.4)
	123	Throned upon the aweful Tree

Matthew 21, 1-13

*	103	All glory, laud, and honour
*	114	Ride on, ride on in majesty
	636	When, his salvation bringing
	639	When Jesus left his Father's throne
	126 †	Give me joy in my heart, keep me praising
	640	Who is he in yonder stall (vv. 6-10 only)

General Choice	* 87	Approach, my soul, the mercy-seat
	* 90	Lord, in this thy mercy's day
	102	Alone thou goest forth, O Lord
	* 104	Glory be to Jesus
	105	Nature with open volume stands
	108	O dearest Lord, thy sacred head
	* 109	O sacred head, surrounded
	112	Sing, my tongue, the glorious battle
	* 116	The royal banners forward go
	245	The heavenly Word proceeding forth
	247	Thee we adore, O hidden Saviour, thee
	* 279	Lift up your heads, ye gates of brass
	380	My God, I love thee; not because
	* 388	Praise to the Holiest in the height
	* 392	There is a green hill far away
	* 570	Just as I am, without one plea
	661	Jesus, and shall it ever be
	680	Ah, holy Jesu, how hast thou offended
	81 †	Peter feared the Cross for himself and his Master
	130 †	God everlasting, wonderful and holy
	154 †	Lord Christ, we praise your sacrifice
	184 †	To mock your reign, O dearest Lord
	190 †	Were you there when they crucified my Lord?

THE MONDAY IN HOLY WEEK

Psalm	55, 1-8 (1-7) *or* 55, 9-15 (8-15)
Old Testament	Isaiah 42, 1-7
Epistle	Hebrews 2, 9-18

*	369	Hail, thou once-despised Jesus!
	366	Glory, glory everlasting
*	373	In the Name of Jesus

Gospel (Year 1)   Matthew 26, 1-30

	245	The heavenly Word proceeding forth
	237	Now, my tongue, the mystery telling
*	570	Just as I am, without one plea

Gospel (Year 2)   Luke 22, 1-38

	245	The heavenly Word proceeding forth
	237	Now, my tongue, the mystery telling
*	570	Just as I am, without one plea
	195 †	Where love and loving-kindness dwell

General Choice   Any of the Hymns in the Passiontide and Holy Week Section (99-117)

THE TUESDAY IN HOLY WEEK

Psalm	55, 18-26 (17-25) *or* 13
Old Testament	Isaiah 49, 1-6
Epistle	Hebrews 8, 1-6

	401	Where high the heavenly temple stands
*	242	Once, only once, and once for all

Gospel (Year 1)   Matthew 26, 31-75

	117	When my love to Christ grows weak
	560	Lord teach us how to pray aright
	565	Shepherd divine, our wants relieve
	81 †	Peter feared the Cross for himself and his Master

Gospel (Year 2)	Luke 22, 39-71

        117   When my love to Christ grows weak
        560   Lord, teach us how to pray aright
        565   Shepherd divine, our wants relieve
        81 †   Peter feared the Cross for himself and his Master

General Choice   Any of the Hymns in the Passiontide and Holy Week
Section (99-117)

THE WEDNESDAY IN HOLY WEEK

Psalm   54   *or*   102, 1-11

Old Testament   Isaiah 50, 4-9a

Epistle   1 Peter 2, 19-25

        537   Lord, as to thy dear Cross we flee
        505   O happy band of pilgrims

Gospel (Year 1)   Matthew 27, 1-56

        381   My song is love unknown
        154 † Lord Christ, we praise you for your sacrifice
        184 † To mock your reign, O dearest Lord
        123   Throned upon the aweful Tree
        29 †   Forgive our sins as we forgive

Gospel (Year 2)   Luke 23, 1-49

        381   My song is love unknown
        122   O word of pity, for our pardon pleading
        121   O perfect life of love!
    * 369   Hail, thou once despised Jesus!
    * 577   Hark, my soul! it is the Lord

General Choice   Any of the Hymns in the Passiontide and Holy Week
Section (99-117)

MAUNDY THURSDAY

Theme : The Lord's Supper

Psalm	116, 11-18 (11-16) *or* 26
Old Testament	Exodus 12, 1-14
Epistle	1 Corinthians 11, 23-29

     * 241   O Thou what at thy Eucharist didst pray
     114 †   Christians, lift your hearts and voices

Gospel	John 13, 1-15

     101 †   An upper room did our Lord prepare
     237   Now, my tongue, the mystery telling
     156 †   Lord God, your love has called us here

General Choice

Any of the Hymns in the Holy Communion

Section (213-251) or any of the following :-

       8 †   As the disciples, when thy Son had left them
     19 †   Dear Lord, to you again our gifts we bring
     94 †   The Son of God proclaim
   106 †   Christ is the heavenly food that gives
   110 †   Christian people, raise your song
   113 †   Christians, lift up your hearts, and make this
                        a day of rejoicing
   132 †   God is love, and where true love is,
                        God himself is there
   140 †   I come with joy to meet my Lord
   144 †   Jesus, we thus obey
   147 †   Let us break bread together on our knees
   196 †   Who are we who stand and sing

GOOD FRIDAY

Theme : The Death of Christ

Psalm	22, 14-22 (14-21) *or* 69, 17-23 (17-22)
Old Testament	Isaiah 52, 13- 53, 12

     97   When wounded sore the stricken soul

Epistle	Hebrews 10, 1-25 (or 12-22)
	* 214 And now, O Father, mindful of the love (vv.1-3)
	* 242 Once, only once, and once for all
	Hebrews 4, 14-16 & 5, 7-9
	401 Where high the heavenly temple stands
	* 330 Father, of heaven, whose love profound
	197 † With joy we meditate the grace
Gospel	John 18, 1- 19, 37 (or 19, 1-37)
	* 392 There is a green hill far away
	81 † Peter feared the Cross for himself and his Master
	* 369 Hail, thou once despised Jesus!
	* 109 O sacred head, surrounded
General Choice	Any of the hymns in the Passiontide and Holy Week Section (99-117) or the following :-
	190 † Were you there when they crucified my Lord?

EASTER EVE

Psalm	16, 8-11 (9-12)
	23
	* 510 The Lord my pasture shall prepare
	* 511 The Lord's my Shepherd, I'll not want
	* 512 The King of love my Shepherd is
Old Testament	Job 14, 1-14
	* 582 Jesu, lover of my soul
Epistle	1 Peter 3, 17-22
	125 It is finished! blessed Jesu
Gospel	Matthew 27, 57-66
	John 2, 18-22
	457 Jesus, where'er thy people meet
	* 439 Lights's abode, celestial Salem

EASTER DAY

Theme   :   The Resurrection of Christ

Psalm	118, 14-24
	116 † Come, let us with our Lord arise
	38 O Day of rest and gladness
	114
	Easter Anthems
	* 132 Hallelujah! Hallelujah!
Old Testament	Isaiah 12
	Exodus 14, 15-22
	131 Come, ye faithful, raise the strain
	127 At the Lamb's high feast we sing
	Isaiah 43, 16-21
	131 Come, ye faithful, raise the strain
For the Epistle	Revelation 1, 10-18
	200 † You, living Christ, our eyes behold
Epistle	1 Corinthians 15, 12-20
	* 141 This joyful Eastertide
	Colossians 3, 1-11
	69 † Now is eternal life
	9 † Awake, awake: fling off the night!
	277 In Christ there is no east or west
Gospel	Matthew 28, 1-10
	135 Light's glittering morn bedecks the sky
	John 20, 1-10
	118 † Early morning. 'Come, prepare him'
	185 † Walking in a garden

Gospel (cont.)   Mark 16, 1-8

  136   O sons and daughters, let us sing! (vv.1-3 & 8)

General Choice   Any of the Hymns in the Easter Section (126-145)

              or any of the following :-

  *   3   Christ, whose glory fills the skies
  * 234   Lord, enthroned in heavenly splendour
  * 326   I bind unto myself today   (vv. 1-2 & 8-9)
  * 364   Crown him with many crowns
  * 368   Hark ten thousand voices sounding
  * 453   Jesu, stand among us
     508   Peace, perfect peace, in this dark world of sin?
  * 556   Through the night of doubt and sorrow
     615   It is the joyful Easter-time
      58 †   Lord Jesus Christ
      95 †   Thine be the glory, risen, conquering Son
     104 †   Away with gloom, away with doubt
     110 †   Christian people, raise your song
     122 †   Finished the strife of battle now
     154 †   Lord Christ, we praise your sacrifice
     168 †   Now the green blade riseth from the buried grain

THE MONDAY IN EASTER WEEK

Psalm	Easter Anthems
	* 132 Hallelujah! Hallelujah!
	Te Deum (Part 2)
Old Testament	Isaiah 42, 10-16
Epistle	1 Peter 1, 1-12
	* 139 The Day of Resurrection
Gospel	Luke 24, 13-35

*	10	Abide with me; fast falls the eventide
	490	Abide among us with thy grace
	220	Come, risen Lord, and deign to be our guest
	29	The day hath now an ending
*	608	God is always near me
	597	O Jesu, King most wonderful (Part 2 only)

THE TUESDAY IN EASTER WEEK

Psalm	16, 8-11 (8-12)
	30
Old Testament	Micah 7, 7-20
Epistle	1 Peter 1, 13-25
	* 493 Children of the heavenly King
	69 † Now is eternal life
Gospel	Luke 24, 36-49

	129	Christ the Lord is risen again
	138	Take heart, friends and neighbours
	140	The happy morn is come
*	143	The whole bright world rejoices now

THE WEDNESDAY IN EASTER WEEK

Psalm	111
	112
Old Testament	1 Kings 17, 17-24
	* 402 Breathe on me, Breath of God
Epistle	1 Peter 2, 1-10
	449 Christ is our corner stone
	259 Christ is made the sure foundation
	* 556 How sweet the Name of Jesus sounds
	146 † Let the Lord's People, heart and voice uniting
	125 † Forth in the peace of Christ we go
Gospel	John 20, 24-31
	167 O thou who didst with love untold
	136 O sons and daughters, let us sing!
	* 453 Jesu, stand among us
	586 Jesus, these eyes have never seen
	244 Soul, array thyself with gladness

THE THURSDAY IN EASTER WEEK

Psalm	113
	114
Old Testament	Jeremiah 31, 1-14
Epistle	1 Peter 2, 11-25
	189 † We turn to you, O God of every nation
	63 † Lord of lords and King eternal
	537 Lord, as to thy dear Cross we flee
	* 505 O happy band of pilgrims
Gospel	John 21, 1-14
	* 597 Jesu, the very thought of thee (Part I)

THE FRIDAY IN EASTER WEEK

Psalm	115	
	116, 1-9	
	* 141	This joyful Eastertide
Old Testament	Ezekiel 37, 1-14	
	* 402	Breathe on me, Breath of God
	409	O Spirit of the living God
Epistle	1 Peter 3, 1-12	
	291	Our Father, by whose name
	149 †	Life is great! So sing about it
Gospel	John 21, 15-17	
	* 577	Hark, my soul! it is the Lord
	* 584	Jesu, my Lord, my God, my all
	176	Thou art the Christ, O Lord

THE SATURDAY IN EASTER WEEK

Psalm	118	
	116 †	Come, let us with our Lord arise
Old Testament	Job 14, 1-14	
	* 582	Jesu, lover of my soul
Epistle	1 Peter 4, 1-11	
	518	Help us to help each other, Lord
	* 517	Gracious Spirit, Holy Ghost
Gospel	John 21, 20-25	
	69	Word supreme, before creation

THE FIRST SUNDAY AFTER EASTER
(LOW SUNDAY)

Themes	:	The Upper Room	(Year 1)
		The Bread of Life	(Year 2)

YEAR 1

Psalm

145, 1-12

346   All creatures of our God and King

Old Testament

Exodus 15, 1-11

131   Come, ye faithful, raise the strain
127   At the Lamb's high feast we sing

Epistle

1 Peter 1, 3-9

* 139   The day of Resurrection!

Gospel

John 20, 19-29

136   O sons and daughters, let us sing!
167   O Thou who didst with love untold
* 453   Jesu, stand among us
586   Jesus, these eyes have never seen
508   Peace, perfect peace, in this dark world of sin

General Choice

*   36   On this day, the first of days
129   Christ the Lord is risen again
130   'Christ the Lord is risen today'
134   Jesus lives: thy terrors now
135   Light's glittering morn bedecks the sky
220   Come, risen Lord, and deign to be our guest
* 236   O God, unseen, yet ever near
247   Thee we adore , O hidden Saviour, thee
* 402   Breathe on me, Breath of God
* 455   Great Shepherd of thy people, hear
77 †   O holy Father, God most dear
79 †   O Lord, we long to see your face
91 †   The first day of the week
101 †   An upper room did our Lord prepare

YEAR 2

Psalm	34, 1-10	
	* 485	Through all the changing scenes of life
	114 †	Christians, lift your hearts and voices
Old Testament	Exodus 16, 2-15	
Epistle	1 Corinthians 15, 53-58	
	* 10	Abide with me; fast falls the eventide
	130	'Christ the Lord is risen today'
	95 †	Thine be the glory, risen, conquering Son
	* 142	The strife is o'er, the battle done
	137	Our Lord Christ hath risen
	134	Jesus lives: thy terrors now
Gospel	John 6, 32-40	
	217	Bread of heaven, on thee we feed
	* 219	Bread of the world, in mercy broken
	574	Come unto me, ye weary
	227	I hunger and I thirst
	* 229	Jesu, thou Joy of loving hearts
	* 236	O God, unseen, yet ever near
General Choice	127	At the Lamb's high feast we sing
	* 132	Hallelujah! Hallelujah!
	* 139	The day of Resurrection!
	* 141	This joyful Eastertide
	223	Father, we thank thee who hast planted
	227	I hunger and I thirst
	* 234	Lord, enthroned in heavenly splendour
	244	Soul, array thyself with gladness
	* 496	Guide me, O thou great Jehovah
	507	Oft in danger, oft in woe
	8 †	As thy disciples, when thy Son had left them
	77 †	O holy Father, God most dear
	106 †	Christ is the heavenly food that gives
	110 †	Christian people, raise your song
	130 †	God everlasting, wonderful and holy
	144 †	Jesus, we thus obey
	147 †	Let us break bread together on our knees

THE SECOND SUNDAY AFTER EASTER

Themes   :   The Emmaus Road   (Year 1)
              The Good Shepherd   (Year 2)

YEAR 1

Psalm   111

Old Testament   Isaiah 25, 6-9

                127   At the Lamb's high feast we sing
                137   Our Lord Christ hath risen

For the Epistle   Revelation 19, 6-9

                127   At the Lamb's high feast we sing
                129   Christ the Lord is risen again
        * 384   The head that once was crowned with thorns
                340   The Lord is King! lift up thy voice

Gospel   Luke 24, 13-35

        * 10   Abide with me; fast falls the eventide
              490   Abide among us with thy grace
              220   Come, risen Lord, and deign to be our guest
                29   The day hath now an ending
        * 608   God is always near me
              597   O Jesu, King most wonderful (Part 2 only)

General Choice   144   Ye choirs of new Jerusalem
        * 234   Lord, enthroned in heavenly splendour
              395   Thou art the Way: to thee alone
        * 437   Jerusalem the golden
            98 †   We have a gospel to proclaim
           140 †   I come with joy to meet my Lord

YEAR 2

Psalm	23	
	510	The Lord my pasture shall prepare
	* 511	The Lord's my Shepherd, I'll not want
	* 512	The King of love my Shepherd is
Old Testament	Ezekiel 34, 7-15	
Epistle	1 Peter 5, 1-11	
	258	Pour out thy Spirit from on high
	522	Be thou my guardian and my guide
Gospel	John 10, 7-16	
	623	Loving Shepherd of thy sheep
	670	Souls of men, why will ye scatter

General Choice

* 455	Great Shepherd of thy people, hear
457	Jesus, where'er thy people meet
* 495	Faithful Shepherd, feed me
* 596	How sweet the Name of Jesus sounds
* 621	Jesus, tender Shepherd, hear me
* 627	See, the good Shepherd, Jesus, stands
680	Ah, holy Jesu, how hast thou offended
14 †	Christ, who knows all his sheep
49 †	Jesus our Lord, our King and our God
83 †	Praise the Lord, rise up rejoicing
141 †	In Adam we have all been one

THE THIRD SUNDAY AFTER EASTER

Themes : The Lakeside   (Year 1)
                The Resurrection and the Life (Year 2)

YEAR 1

Psalm   16

Old Testament   Isaiah 61, 1-7

*	45	Hark the glad sound! the Saviour comes
	418	Hail to the Lord's Anointed
*	284	Thou whose almighty word

Epistle   1 Corinthians 15, 1-11

*	142	The strife is o'er, the battle done
	134	Jesus lives: thy terrors now

Gospel   John 21, 1-14

*	597	Jesu, the very thought of thee (Part 1)

General Choice

	130	'Christ the Lord is risen today'
*	132	Hallelujah! Hallelujah!
	135	Light's glittering morn bedecks the sky
	215	Author of life divine
*	233	My God, and is thy table spread
*	370	Hallelujah! Sing to Jesus!
	535	'Lift up your hearts!' We lift them, Lord, to the
*	575	Dear Lord and Father of mankind
	94 †	The Son of God proclaim
	95 †	Thine be the glory, risen, conquering Son
	98 †	We have a gospel to proclaim
	116 †	Come, let us with our Lord arise
	168 †	Now the green blade riseth from the buried grain
	200 †	You, living Christ, our eyes behold

YEAR 2

Psalm   30

Old Testament   1 Kings 17, 17-24

                           * 402   Breathe on me, Breath of God

Epistle   Colossians 3, 1-11

                           9 †   Awake, awake: fling off the night!
                        69 †   Now is eternal life

Gospel   John 11, 17-27

                        69 †   Now is eternal life

General Choice
                * 36   On this day, the first of days
                  134   Jesus lives: thy terrors now
                  395   Thou art the Way: to thee alone
                  438   Let saints on earth in concert sing
                * 544   O Jesus, I have promised
                 95 † Thine be the glory, risen, conquering Son
               104 † Away with gloom, away with doubt
               116 † Come, let us with our Lord arise
               143 † Jesus, my Lord, let me be near you
               181 † There in God's garden stands the tree of wisdom

THE FOURTH SUNDAY AFTER EASTER

Themes :   The Charge to Peter   (Year 1)
             The Way, the Truth and the Life   (Year 2)

YEAR 1

Psalm   33, 1-12

Old Testament   Isaiah 62, 1-5

                      7 †   As the bridegroom to his chosen

For the Epistle   Revelation 3, 14-22

               593   O Jesu, thou art standing

Gospel   John 21, 15-22

          * 577   Hark, my soul! it is the Lord
          * 584   Jesu, my Lord, my God, my all
            176   Thou art the Christ, O Lord
          * 166   Jesus calls us! o'er the tumult
            258   Pour out thy Spirit from on high
           49 †   Jesus our Lord, our King and our God

General Choice   * 495   Faithful Shepherd, feed me
          * 544   O Jesus, I have promised
          * 554   Take up thy cross, the Saviour said
          * 570   Just as I am, without one plea
           12 †   Christ is the King! O friends rejoice
         125 †   Forth in the peace of Christ we go
         176 †   Rise and hear! The Lord is speaking

YEAR 2

Psalm 37, 23-32

Old Testament Proverbs 4, 10-19

Epistle 2 Corinthians 4, 13- 5, 5

*	439	Light's abode, celestial Salem
	440	My soul, there is a country
	670	Souls of men, why will ye scatter

Gospel John 14, 1-11

	395	Thou art the Way: to thee alone
*	553	Thine for ever! God of love
	79 †	O Lord, we long to see your face
	564	Prayer is the soul's sincere desire
	524	Brothers, joining hand to hand
	251	We pray thee, heavenly Father
	107 †	Christ is the world's light, he and none other
*	501	Lead us, heavenly Father, lead us

General Choice

	316	Rejoice, O land, in God thy might
	365	Give to our God immortal praise
*	437	Jerusalem the golden
	441	O what the joy and the glory must be
	444	Sing Hallelujah forth in duteous praise
	445	There is a land of pure delight
	586	Jesus, these eyes have never seen
	49 †	Jesus our Lord, our King and our God!
	65 †	Lord that descendedst, Holy Child
	79 †	O Lord, we long to see your face

85

THE FIFTH SUNDAY AFTER EASTER
(ROGATION SUNDAY)

Theme   :   Going to the Father

YEAR 1

Psalm	84	
	456	How lovely are thy dwellings fair!
	459	Pleasant are thy courts above
	166 †	Now from the altar of our hearts
Old Testament	Hosea 6, 1-6	
Epistle	1 Corinthians 15, 21-28	
	* 132	Hallelujah! Hallelujah!
	134	Jesus lives: thy terrors now
	137	Our Lord Christ hath risen
Gospel	John 16, 25-33	
	340	The Lord is King! lift up thy voice
	397	Rejoice, the Lord is King!

YEAR 2

Psalm	15	
Old Testament	Deutronomy 34	
	445	There is a land of pure delight
Epistle	Romans 8, 28-39	
	* 364	Crown him with many crowns (vv. 1, 3, 4 & 6)
	568	Jesus, thy Blood and righteousness
Gospel	John 16, 12-24	
	* 405	Come, gracious Spirit, heavenly Dove
	558	Come, my soul, thy suit prepare

General Choice	134	Jesus lives: thy terrors now
	* 141	This joyful Eastertide
	320	Alone with none but thee, my God
	* 344	Immortal, invisible, God only wise
	354	Praise the Lord! ye heavens adore him
	365	Give to our God immortal praise
	* 493	Children of the heavenly King
	499	Jesus, still lead on
	586	Jesus, these eyes have never seen
	* 592	Nearer, my God, to thee
	39 †	Have faith in God, my heart
	69 †	Now is eternal life

Rogation Hymns	146	O Jesus, crowned with all renown
	* 147	Lord, in thy Name thy servants plead
	301	God, whose farm is all creation
	303	Holy is the seed-time, when the buried grain
	* 506	O God of Bethel, by whose hand
	124 †	For the fruits of his creation
	177 †	Sent forth by God's blessing, our true faith confessing

ROGATION DAYS - MONDAY

Psalm	107, 1-9
	121
	* 513 To Zion's hill I lift my eyes
Old Testament	Job 28, 1-11
Epistle	2 Thessalonians 3, 6-13
	* 268 Lord of the living harvest
Gospel	Matthew 6, 1-15
	560 Lord, teach us how to pray aright
	561 Lord, when we bend before thy throne
	565 Shepherd divine, our wants relieve
	539 My God, my Father, make me strong

ROGATION DAYS - TUESDAY

Psalm	*As appointed for Monday (above)*
Old Testament	Deuteronomy 8, 1-10
Epistle	Philippians 4, 4-7
	397 Rejoice, the Lord is King
	476 Fill thou my life, O Lord my God
	567 There is no sorrow, Lord, too light
	* 679 What a friend we have in Jesus

ROGATION DAYS - WEDNESDAY

Psalm	*As appointed for Monday (above)*
Old Testament	1 Kings 8, 35-40
Epistle	1 John 5, 12-15
	69 † Now is eternal life
Gospel	Mark 11, 22-24
	39 † Have faith in God, my heart

THE ASCENSION DAY

Theme   :   The Ascension of Christ

Psalm	8	
	198 †	With wonder, Lord, we see your works
	21, 1-7	
Old Testament	Daniel 7, 9-14	
	* 391	Ten thousand times ten thousand
	139 †	How shall I sing that majesty
For the Epistle	Acts 1, 1-11	
	152	Thou art gone up on high
	* 150	Hail the day that sees him rise
	148	Christ, above all glory seated
Gospel	Matthew 28, 16-20	
	273	For my sake and the gospel's, go
	* 477	Ye servants of God, your Master proclaim
	409	O Spirit of the living God
	282	Spread, O spread, thou mighty word
	277	In Christ there is no east or west
General Choice	* 153	See the Conqueror mounts in triumph
	* 154	The golden gates are lifted up
	155	The Lord ascendeth up on high
	* 359	All hail the power of Jesu's Name
	* 369	Hail, thou once-despised Jesus!
	* 370	Hallelujah! Sing to Jesus
	* 373	In the Name of Jesus
	* 384	The head that once was crowned with thorns
	616	Jesu, high in glory
	644	Let me be with thee where thou art
	65 †	Lord that descendedst, Holy Child
	200 †	You, living Christ, our eyes behold

THE SUNDAY AFTER ASCENSION DAY

(The Sixth Sunday after Easter)

Theme : The Ascension of Christ

YEAR 1

Psalm	24	
	279	Lift up your heads, ye gates of brass
	413	Lift up your heads, ye mighty gates
	* 154	The golden gates are lifted up
	149	Golden harps are sounding
	* 150	Hail the day that sees him rise
	* 153	See the Conqueror mounts in triumph
Old Testament	Daniel 7, 9-14	
	* 391	Ten thousand times ten thousand
	139 †	How shall I sing that majesty
Epistle	Ephesians 1, 15-23	
	378	Look, ye saints, the sight is glorious
	364	Crown him with many crowns (vv.1 & 4-6)
	* 359	All hail the power of Jesu's Name
Gospel	Luke 24, 45-53	
	148	Christ, above all glory seated!
	* 384	The head that once was crowned with thorns

YEAR 2

Psalm	47	
Old Testament	2 Kings 2, 1-15	
Epistle	Ephesians 4, 1-13	
	* 431	Thy hand, O God, has guided
	155	The Lord ascendeth up on high
	257	O thou who makest souls to shine
	401	Where high the heavenly temple stands

Gospel

Luke 24, 45-53

   148   Christ, above all glory seated
* 384   The head that once was crowned with thorns

General Choice

* 150   Hail the day that sees him rise
  259   Christ is made the sure foundation
* 344   Immortal, invisible, God only wise
  362   Come, let us join our cheerful songs
  363   Come, ye faithful, raise the anthem
  365   Give to our God immortal praise
* 369   Hail, thou once-despised Jesus!
* 370   Hallelujah! Sing to Jesus!
* 373   In the Name of Jesus
* 376   Lift high the Cross, the love of Christ proclaim
  397   Rejoice, the Lord is King!
  418   Hail to the Lord's Anointed
* 421   Jesus shall reign where'er the sun
  444   Sing Hallelujah forth in duteous praise
* 477   Ye servants of God, you Master proclaim
  478   King of glory, King of peace
    1 †   A Man there lived in Galilee
  65 †   Lord that descendedst, Holy Child
165 †   New songs of celebration render
197 †   With joy we meditate the grace

PENTECOST   (WHITSUNDAY)

Theme : The Gift of the Spirit

YEAR 1

Psalm   122

Old Testament Genesis 11, 1-9

For the Epistle Acts 2, 1-11

    159 Lord God the Holy Ghost
    162 Spirit of mercy, truth, and power
    26 † Filled with the Spirit's power, with one accord
    111 † Christians, lift up your hearts, and make this
        a day of rejoicing
    171 † On the day of Pentecost
    23 † Father, Lord of all creation

Gospel   John 14, 15-26

    * 161 Our blest Redeemer, ere he breathed
    * 403 Come down, O Love divine

YEAR 2

Psalm   36, 5-10

Old Testament Exodus 19, 16-25

For the Epistle Acts 2, 1-11

    159 Lord God the Holy Ghost
    162 Spirit of mercy, truth, and power
    26 † Filled with the Spirit's power, with one accord
    111 † Christians, lift up your hearts, and make this
        a day of rejoicing
    171 † On the day of Pentecost
    23 † Father, Lord of all creation

Gospel   John 20, 19-23

    * 453 Jesu, stand among us
    * 402 Breathe on me, Breath of God

General Choice

*	156	Come, Holy Ghost, our souls inspire
	157	Come, thou Holy Spirit, come
	158	Creator Spirit, by whose aid
	160	O Holy Ghost, thy people bless
	165	We give immortal praise
	265	O Lord of heaven and earth and sea
	404	Holy Spirit, hear us
*	405	Come, gracious Spirit, heavenly Dove
	406	Holy Spirit, truth divine
	407	Love of the Father, Love of God the Son
	408	O King enthroned on high
	409	O Spirit of the living God
	461	Spirit divine, attend our prayer
	492	All my hope on God is founded
	517	Gracious Spirit, Holy Ghost
	528	Eternal Ruler of the ceaseless round
	648	O for a closer walk with God
	98 †	We have a gospel to proclaim
	138 †	Holy Spirit, come, confirm us
	145 †	Let every Christian pray
	170 †	Of all the Spirit's gifts to me
	182 †	There's a spirit in the air
	193 †	When Jesus came to Jordan

TRINITY SUNDAY
(The First Sunday after Pentecost)
Theme   :   The Holy Trinity

Psalm

93

97

340   The Lord is King!   lift up thy voice

Old Testament

Isaiah 6, 1-8

* 328   Bright the vision that delighted
  231   Let all mortal flesh keep silence
* 474   Angel voices, ever singing
  199 † Ye watchers and ye holy ones

Epistle

Ephesians 1, 3-14

502   May the grace of Christ our Saviour
 23 † Father, Lord of all creation

Gospel

John 14, 8-17

107 † Christ is the world's light, he and none other

General Choice

Appropriate for use on Trinity Sunday

* 335   My God, how wonderful thou art
  339   God is a Name my soul adores
* 352   O worship the King all-glorious above
  139 † How shall I sing that majesty
  160 † Lord of the boundless curves of space

THE SECOND SUNDAY AFTER PENTECOST

| Themes | : | The People of God | (Year 1) |
| | | The Church's Unity and Fellowship | (Year 2) |

YEAR 1

Psalm   95, 1-7

Old Testament Exodus 19, 1-6

Epistle   1 Peter 2, 1-10

	449	Christ is our corner-stone
	259	Christ is made the sure foundation
*	596	How sweet the Name of Jesus sounds
	146 †	Let the Lord's People, heart and voice uniting
	125 †	Forth in the peace of Christ we go

Gospel   John 15, 1-5

| * | 415 | Glorious things of thee are spoken |

General Choice

*	32	The day thou gavest, Lord, is ended
	160	O Holy Ghost, thy people bless
	257	O thou who makest souls to shine
	258	Pour out thy Spirit from on high
*	430	The Church's one foundation
*	431	Thy hand, O God, has guided
*	506	O God of Bethel, by whose hand
	528	Eternal Ruler of the ceaseless round
	113 †	Christians, lift up your hearts, and make this a day of rejoicing
	131 †	God is here; as we his people
	146 †	Let the Lord's People, heart and voice uniting
	186 †	We are your people
	196 †	Who are we who stand and sing?

YEAR 2

Psalm   135, 1-6

Old Testament 2 Samuel 7, 4-16

| | 464 | To thy temple I repair |
| * | 465 | We love the place, O God |

For the Epistle   Acts 2, 37-47

          409   O Spirit of the living God
          277   In Christ there is no east or west
          112 †   Christians, lift up your hearts, and make this
                        a day of rejoicing

Gospel   Luke 14, 15-24

     * 233   My God, and is thy table spread
       419   Happy are they, they that love God

General Choice   220   Come, risen Lord, and deign to be our guest
              223   Father, we thank thee who hast planted
          * 241   O thou who at thy Eucharist didst pray
              270   Christ is the world's true Light
          * 411   City of God, how broad and far
          * 421   Jesus shall reign where'er the sun
          * 427   Onward, Christian soldiers
          * 430   The Church's one foundation
          * 431   Thy hand, O God, has guided
              438   Let saints on earth in concert sing
          * 455   Great Shepherd of thy people, hear
              518   Help us to help each other, Lord
              524   Brothers, joining hand to hand
              528   Eternal Ruler of the ceaseless round
              551   Son of God, eternal Saviour
          * 556   Through the night of doubt and sorrow
           12 †   Christ is the King! O friends rejoice
           23 †   Father, Lord of all Creation
           26 †   Filled with the Spirit's power, with one accord
           47 †   Jesus, Lord, we look to thee
           53 †   Lord Christ, the Father's mighty Son
           63 †   Lord of lords and King eternal
          132 † God is love, and where true love is, God himself is there
          140 † I come with joy to meet my Lord
          145 † Let every Christian pray
          148 † Let us talents and tongues emply
          195 † Where love and loving-kindness dwell

THE THIRD SUNDAY AFTER PENTECOST

Themes : The Life of the Baptized (Year 1)
The Church's Confidence in Christ (Year 2)

YEAR 1

Psalm 44, 1-9

Old Testament Deuteronomy 6, 17-25

Epistle Romans 6, 3-11

361	Conquering kings their titles take
664	My God, accept my heart this day

Gospel John 15, 5-11

502	May the grace of Christ our Saviour
* 590	Love Divine, all loves excelling
490	Abide among us with thy grace

General Choice

* 132	Hallelujah! Hallelujah!
277	In Christ there is no east or west
* 322	Be thou my vision, O Lord of my heart
* 402	Breathe on me, Breath of God
* 430	The Church's one foundation
* 465	We love the place, O God
476	Fill thou my life, O Lord my God
518	Help us to help each other, Lord
* 544	O Jesus, I have promised
644	Let me be with thee where thou art
656	Come, thou fount of every blessing
683	Jesu, priceless treasure
9 †	Awake, awake: fling off the night!
12 †	Christ is the King! O friends rejoice
69 †	Now is eternal life
109 †	Christ, when for us you were baptized
112 †	Christians, lift up your hearts, and make this a day of rejoicing
143 †	Jesus, my Lord, let me be near you
179 †	'The kingdom is upon you!'
186 †	We are your people
193 †	When Jesus came to Jordan

YEAR 2

Psalm   150

*	342	Let all the world in every corner sing
	480	O praise ye the Lord! Praise him in the Height

Old Testament   Deuteronomy 8, 11-20

	538	Lord, be thy word my rule

For the Epistle   Acts 4, 8-12

	259	Christ is made the sure foundation
	449	Christ is our corner-stone
	361	Conquering kings their titles take

Gospel   Luke 8, 41-56

	662	Jesus Christ is passing by
*	582	Jesu, lover of my soul
	547	Put thou thy trust in God

General Choice

	270	Christ is the world's true Light
*	369	Hail, thou once-despised Jesus!
*	373	In the Name of Jesus
*	376	Lift high the Cross, the love of Christ proclaim
*	382	O for a thousand tongues to sing
*	384	The head that once was crowned with thorns
	399	To the Name of our salvation
	401	Where high the heavenly temple stands
	416	God of Eternity, Lord of the ages
*	427	Onward, Christian soldiers
*	477	Ye servants of God, your Master proclaim
	492	All my hope on God is founded
*	548	Soldiers of Christ, arise
	576	Fierce raged the tempest o'er the deep
	594	O Love that wilt not let me go
*	596	How sweet the Name of Jesus sounds
	683	Jesu, priceless treasure
	1 †	A Man there lived in Galilee
	89 †	Tell out, my soul, the greatness of the Lord
	98 †	We have a gospel to proclaim

THE FOURTH SUNDAY AFTER PENTECOST

Themes   :   The Freedom of the Sons of God   (Year 1)
                  The Church's Ministry to the Individual   (Year 2)

YEAR 1

Psalm	63, 1-9	
	595	Thou hidden love of God, whose height
Old Testament	Deuteronomy 7, 6-11	
Epistle	Galatians 3, 23- 4, 7	
	277	In Christ there is no east or west
	270	Christ is the world's true Light
	265	O Lord of heaven and earth and sea
	* 501	Lead us, heavenly Father, lead us
Gospel	John 15, 12-17	
	* 387	O the deep, deep love of Jesus
	386	O Love, who formedst me to wear
General Choice	265	O Lord of heaven and earth and sea
	* 382	O for a thousand tongues to sing
	* 481	Praise, my soul, the King of heaven
	492	All my hope on God is founded
	* 534	Just as I am, thine own to be
	541	O for a heart to praise my God
	14 †	Christ, who knows all his sheep
	47 †	Jesus, Lord, we look to thee
	61 †	Lord of all hopefulness, Lord of all joy
	92 †	The God who rules this earth
	109 †	Christ, when for us you were baptized
	156 †	Lord God, your love has called us here
	192 †	When Christ was lifted from the earth

YEAR 2

Psalm	67	
	* 417	God of mercy, God of grace
Old Testament	Isaiah 63, 7-14	
For the Epistle	Acts 8, 26-38	
	471	Word of the living God
	468	God hath spoken - by his prophets
	472	O Word of God incarnate
	623	Loving Shepherd of thy sheep
	409	O Spirit of the living God
Gospel	Luke 15, 1-10	
	657	Come, ye sinners, poor and wretched
	674	There were ninety and nine that safely lay
	* 512	The King of love my Shepherd is
	* 570	Just as I am, without one plea
	574	Come unto me, ye weary
	* 627	See, the good Shepherd, Jesus, stand
General Choice	86	All ye who seek for sure relief
	* 91	Lord Jesu, think on me
	269	Lord, speak to me, that I may speak
	377	My blessed Saviour, is thy love
	* 382	O for a thousand tongues to sing
	385	O Love, how deep, how broad, how high!
	* 465	We love the place, O God
	510	The Lord my pasture shall prepare
	* 512	The King of love my Shepherd is
	* 534	Just as I am, thine own to be
	559	Come, O thou traveller unknown
	568	Jesus, thy Blood and righteousness
	* 579	I heard the voice of Jesus say
	* 590	Love Divine, all loves excelling
	594	O Love that wilt not let me go
	* 620	Jesus loves me: this I know
	623	Loving Shepherd of thy sheep
	* 669	Take my life, and let it be
	670	Souls of men, why will ye scatter
	673	Tell me the old, old story
	675	Thou didst leave thy throne and thy kingly crown
	143 †	Jesus, my Lord, let me be near you
	152 †	Lord, as I wake I turn to you

THE FIFTH SUNDAY AFTER PENTECOST

Themes : The New Law   (Year 1)
            The Church's Mission to All Men (Year 2)

YEAR 1

Psalm   119, 57-64

Old Testament   Exodus 20, 1-17

Epistle   Ephesians 5, 1-10

	9 †	Awake, awake: fling off the night!
	2	Awake, my soul, and with the sun
	160	O Holy Ghost, thy people bless
	543	O God of truth, whose living word
*	284	Those whose almighty word
*	523	Blest are the pure in heart

Gospel   Matthew 19, 16-26

	551	Son of God, eternal Saviour
	518	Help us to help each other, Lord
	49 †	Jesus our Lord, our King and our God

General Choice

	395	Thou art the Way: to thee alone
	406	Holy Spirit, truth divine
	419	Happy are they, they that love God
	515	Beloved, let us love: love is of God
	517	Gracious Spirit, Holy Ghost
	518	Help us to help each other, Lord
*	523	Blest are the pure in heart
	528	Eternal Ruler of the ceaseless round
	541	O for a heart to praise my God
	134 †	God, who hast caused to be written thy word for our learning
	170 †	Of all the Spirit's gifts to me
	176 †	Rise and hear! The Lord is speaking

YEAR 2

Psalm	119, 89-96	
Old Testament	Ruth 1, 8-17 & 22	
For the Epistle	Acts 11, 4-18	
	* 405	Come, gracious Spirit, heavenly Dove
Gospel	Luke 10, 1-12	
	268	Lord of the living harvest
	281	Lord, her watch thy Church is keeping
	* 477	Ye servants of God, your Master proclaim
	432	Thy kingdom come! on bended knee

General Choice	270	Christ is the world's true Light
	* 274	God is working his purpose out as year succeeds to year
	277	In Christ there is no east or west
	316	Rejoice, O land, in God thy might
	* 333	All people that on earth do dwell
	* 342	Let all the world in every corner sing
	409	O Spirit of the living God
	414	O Lord our God, arise!
	* 417	God of mercy, God of grace
	* 429	Thy kingdom come, O God
	549	Soldiers of the Cross, arise!
	11 †	Christ for the world we sing
	26 †	Filled with the Spirit's power, with one accord
	63 †	Lord of lords and King eternal
	98 †	We have a Gospel to proclaim
	107 †	Christ is the world's light, he and none other
	125 †	Forth in the peace of Christ we go
	145 †	Let every Christian pray
	148 †	Let us talents and tongues employ
	186 †	We are your people
	192 †	When Christ was lifted from the earth
	196 †	Who are we who stand and sing?

THE SIXTH SUNDAY AFTER PENTECOST

Theme   :   The New Man

YEAR 1

Psalm   112

Old Testament   Exodus 24, 3-11

Epistle   Colossians 3, 12-17

	343	Songs of praise the angels sang
	555	Teach me, my God and King
	47 †	Jesus, Lord, we look to thee
*	474	Angel voices, ever singing
*	479	Now thank we all our God

Gospel   Luke 15, 11-32

	451	Father, again in Jesus' name we meet
*	330	Father, of heaven, whose love profound
*	481	Praise, my soul, the King of heaven
*	225	I am not worthy, Holy Lord

YEAR 2

Psalm   1

Old Testament   Micah 6, 1-8

	99 †	What does the Lord require

Epistle   Ephesians 4, 17-32

	9 †	Awake, awake: fling off the night!

Gospel   Mark 10, 46-52

	66 †	Lord, we are blind; the world of sight
	662	Jesus Christ is passing by
*	91	Lord Jesu, think on me
*	225	I am not worthy, Holy Lord
	290	Thou to whom the sick and dying
*	582	Jesu, lover of my soul

General Choice

THE SEVENTH SUNDAY AFTER PENTECOST

Theme : The More Excellent Way

YEAR 1

Psalm   62

Old Testament   Hosea 11, 1-9

371	Immortal love for ever full
381	My song is love unknown

Epistle   1 Corinthians 12, 27- 13, 13

517	Gracious Spirit, Holy Ghost
* 403	Come down, O Love divine

Gospel   Matthew 18, 21-35

537	Lord as to thy dear Cross we flee
29 †	'Forgive our sinds as we forgive'
* 330	Father, of heaven, whose love profound

YEAR 2

Psalm   103, 8-18

* 481	Praise, my soul, the King of heaven
* 482	Praise to the Lord, the Almighty, the King of creation

Old Testament   Deuteronomy 10, 12- 11, 1

99 †	What does the Lord require

Epistle   Romans 8, 1-11

* 330	Father, of heaven, whose love profound
251	We pray thee, heavenly Father

Gospel   Mark 12, 28-34

132 †	God is love, and where true love is, God himself is there
419	Happy are they, they that love God
518	Help us to help each other, Lord

General Choice

	160	O Holy Ghost, thy people bless
	243	Strengthen for service, Lord, the hands
	341	God is Love: let heaven adore him
	371	Immortal love for ever full
	515	Beloved, let us love: love is of God
	540	O brother man! Fold to thy heart thy brother
	541	O for a heart to praise my God
*	577	Hark, my soul! it is the Lord
*	584	Jesu, my Lord, my God, my all
*	590	Love Divine, all loves excelling
	597	O Jesu, King most wonderful (Part 2)
	26 †	Filled with the Spirit's power, with one accord
	28 †	For the healing of the nations
	29 †	'Forgive our sins as we forgive'
	44 †	In humble gratitude, O God
	55 †	Lord Christ, who on thy heart didst bear
	99 †	What does the Lord require
	162 †	Lord, to you we bring our treasure
	170 †	Of all the Spirit's gifts to me
	195 †	Where love and loving-kindness dwell

THE EIGHTH SUNDAY AFTER PENTECOST
Theme : The Fruit of the Spirit

YEAR 1

Psalm   25, 1-10 (1-9)

Old Testament   Ezekiel 36, 24-28

Epistle   Galatians 5, 16-25

                406   Holy Spirit, truth divine
                170 †   Of all the Spirit's gifts to me
                124 †   For the fruits of his creation

Gospel   John 15, 16-27

                517   Gracious Spirit, Holy Ghost
                515   Beloved, let us love: love is of God
                518   Help us to help each other, Lord

YEAR 2

Psalm   27, 1-8   (1-7)

Old Testament   Ezekiel 37, 1- 14

              * 402   Breathe one me, Breath of God
                409   O Spirit of the living God

Epistle   1 Corinthians 12, 4-13

                157   Come, thou Holy Spirit, come

Gospel   Luke 6, 27-38

                182 †   There's a spirit in the air
                540   O brother man! Fold to thy heart thy brother

General Choice

*	156	Come, Holy Ghost, our souls inspire
	157	Come, thou Holy spirit, come
	160	O Holy Ghost, thy people bless
*	161	Our blest Redeemer, ere he breathed
*	403	Come down, O Love divine
*	405	Come, gracious Spirit, heavenly Dove
	461	Spirit divine, attend our prayer
	492	All my hope on God is founded
*	501	Lead us, heavenly Father, lead us
	528	Eternal Ruler of the ceaseless round
*	590	Love Divine, all loves excelling
	26 †	Filled with the Spirit's power, with one accord
	126 †	Give me joy in my heart, keep me praising
	138 †	Holy Spirit, come, confirm us
	145 †	Let every Christian pray
	170 †	Of all the Spirit's gifts to me
	171 †	On the day of Pentecost
	193 †	When Jesus came to Jordan

THE NINTH SUNDAY AFTER PENTECOST
Theme : The Armour of God

YEAR 1

Psalm   18, 1-7

Old Testament Joshua 1, 1-9

           * 556   Through the night of doubt and sorrow
           524   Brothers, joining hand to hand

Epistle   Ephesians 6, 10-20

           * 548   Soldiers of Christ, arise
           549   Soldiers of the Cross, arise!
           * 552   Stand up, stand up for Jesus
           507   Of in danger, oft in woe
           526   Christian, seek not yet repose

Gospel   John 17, 11b-19

           623   Loving Shepherd of thy sheep

YEAR 2

Psalm   18, 32-38   (31-37)

Old Testament 1 Samuel 17, 37-50

           * 498   He who would valiant be
           * 322   Be thou my vision, O Lord of my heart

Epistle   2 Corinthians 6, 3-10

           532   Gracious Father, hear our prayer
           * 530   Fight the good fight with all thy might

Gospel   Mark 9, 14-29

           662   Jesus Christ is passing by

General Choice

*	326	I bind unto myself today
	423	Lord of our life, and God of our salvation
*	427	Onward, Christian soldiers
	473	A safe stronghold our God is still
	528	Eternal Ruler of the ceaseless round
	543	O God of truth, whose living word
	550	Soldiers, who are Christ's below
*	554	Take up thy cross, the Saviour said
	34 †	God of grace and God of glory
	183 †	This day God gives me

THE TENTH SUNDAY AFTER PENTECOST
Theme : The Mind of Christ

YEAR 1

Psalm 71, 1-8 (1-7)

Old Testament Job 42, 1-6

Epistle Philippians 2, 1-11

       * 373   In the Name of Jesus
       4 †   All praise to thee, for thou, O King divine
       * 523   Blest are the pure in heart
       684   O Jesu so meek, O Jesu so kind

Gospel John 13, 1-15

       237   Now, my tongue, the mystery telling
       101 †   An upper room did our Lord prepare
       156 †   Lord God, your love has called us here

YEAR 2

Psalm 73, 23-28

Old Testament 1 Samuel 24, 9-17 (or 1-17)

Epistle Galatians 6, 1-10

       518   Help us to help each other, Lord
       47 †   Jesus, Lord, we look to thee

Gospel Luke 7, 36-50

       29 †   'Forgive our sins as we forgive'
       386   O Love, who formedst me to wear
       377   My blessed Saviour, is thy love
       380   My God, I love thee; not because

General Choice

Theme : The Serving Community

YEAR 1

Psalm	31. 21-27
Old Testament	Isaiah 42, 1-7
	* 45 Hark the glad sound! the Saviour comes
Epistle	2 Corinthians 4, 1-10
	278 Light of them that sit in darkness!
	197 Disposer supreme, and Judge of the earth
	* 284 Thou whose almighty word
	31 † God is Light
Gospel	John 13, 31-35
	518 Help us to help each other, Lord
	517 Gracious Spirit, Holy Ghost
	195 † Where love and loving-kindness dwell

YEAR 2

Psalm	40, 1-7
Old Testament	1 Chronicles 29, 1-9
	551 Son of God, eternal Saviour
	* 465 We love the place, O God
	* 474 Angel voices, ever singing
Epistle	Philippians 1, 1-11
	4 Forth, in thy Name, O Lord I go
Gospel	Matthew 20, 1-16
	* 249 Upon thy table, Lord, we place
	557 Ye servants of the Lord
	* 477 Ye servants of God, your Master proclaim

General Choice

THE TWELFTH SUNDAY AFTER PENTECOST

Theme : The Witnessing Community

YEAR 1

Psalm   96, 1-6

                    280   Let the song go round the earth

Old Testament Isaiah 49, 1-6

Epistle   2 Corinthians 5, 14- 6, 2

                    379   Now to him who loved us, gave us

Gospel   John 17, 20-26

                  * 412   Father of all, from land and sea
                  * 241   O thou who at thy Eucharist didst pray
                    53 †   Lord Christ, the Father's mighty Son
                  * 430   The Church's one foundation

YEAR 2

Psalm   96, 7-13

                  * 466   Worship the Lord in the beauty of holiness

Old Testament Micah 4, 1-5

                    270   Christ is the world's true Light

For the Epistle Acts 17, 22-34

                    457   Jesus, where'er thy people meet
                  * 352   O worship the King all-glorious above
                    351   Lord of beauty, thine the splendour

Gospel   Matthew 5, 13-16

                    278   Light of them that sit in darkness !
                    536   Light of the lonely pilgrim's heart
                    9 †   Awake, awake: fling off the night!

General Choice

THE THIRTEENTH SUNDAY AFTER PENTECOST
Theme : The Suffering Community

YEAR 1

Psalm	31, 1-5 (1-6)
Old Testament	Isaiah 50, 4-9a
For the Epistle	Acts 7, 54 - 8, 1

        340   The Lord is King! lift up thy voice
        195   The Son of God goes forth to war

Gospel   John 16, 1-11

      * 405   Come, gracious Spirit, heavenly Dove

YEAR 2

Psalm	43
Old Testament	Jeremiah 20, 7-11a
For the Epistle	Acts 20, 17-35

      * 429   Thy kingdom come, O God
      258   Pour out thy Spirit from on high

Gospel   Matthew 10, 16-22

      * 403   Come down, O Love divine

THE FOURTEENTH SUNDAY AFTER PENTECOST

Theme : The Family

YEAR 1

Psalm   127

Old Testament   Proverbs 31, 10-31

Epistle   Ephesians 5, 25- 6, 4
                       107   O crucified Redeemer

Gospel   Mark 10, 2-16
                       619   Jesus, Friend of little children
                       631   Thou who once on mother's knee

YEAR 2

Psalm   128

Old Testament   Genesis 45, 1-15

Epistle   Ephesians 3, 14-21
                       291   Our Father, by whose Name
                       74   O God in heaven, whose loving plan

Gospel   Luke 11, 1-13
                       560   Lord, teach us how to pray aright
                       558   Come, my soul, thy suit prepare
                       58 †   Lord Jesus Christ

General Choice

THE FIFTEENTH SUNDAY AFTER PENTECOST

Theme : Those in Authority

YEAR 1

Psalm 82

Old Testament Isaiah 45, 1-7
279 Lift up your heads, ye gates of brass!

Epistle Romans 13, 1-7
317 To thee our God we fly (vv.1-4 & 8-9)

Gospel Matthew 22, 15-22
423 Lord of our life, and God of our salvation
* 429 Thy kingdom come, O God
* 265 O Lord of heaven and earth and sea

YEAR 2

Psalm 20

Old Testament 1 Kings 3, 4-15

Epistle 1 Timothy 2, 1-7
99 † What does the Lord require

Gospel Matthew 14, 1-12
28 † For the healing of the nations
426 Put forth, O God, thy Spirit's might

General Choice

270	Christ is the world's true Light
310	God save our gracious Queen (Northern Ireland only)
316	Rejoice, O land, in God thy might
317	To thee our God we fly (vv.1-4 & 8-9)
340	The Lord is King! lift up thy voice
428	Rise up, O men of God!
528	Eternal Ruler of the ceaseless round
529	Father, who on man dost shower
557	Ye servants of the Lord
22(ii)†	Father all-loving, thou rulest in majesty
28 †	For the healing of the nations
35 †	God of love and truth and beauty
63 †	Lord of lords and King eternal
72 †	O Day of God, draw nigh
99 †	What does the Lord require
189 †	We turn to you, O God of every nation

THE SIXTEENTH SUNDAY AFTER PENTECOST

Theme : The Neighbour

YEAR 1

Psalm
34, 1-10

     * 485   Through all the changing scenes of life
     114 †   Christians, lift your hearts and voices

Old Testament
Leviticus 19, 9-18

Epistle
Romans 12, 9-21

     29 †   'Forgive our sins as we forgive'
     540   O brother man! Fold to thy heart thy brother
     524   Brothers, joining hand to hand

Gospel
Luke 10, 25-37

     518   Help us to help each other, Lord
     290   Thou to whom the sick and dying

YEAR 2

Psalm
34, 11-18

     566   There is an eye that never sleeps

Old Testament
Deuteronomy 15, 7-11

Epistle
1 John 4, 15-21

     341   God is love: let heaven adore him

Gospel
Luke 16, 19-31

     48 †   Jesus, my Lord, how rich thy grace
     100 †   When I needed a neighbour, were you there?

THE SEVENTEENTH SUNDAY AFTER PENTECOST

Theme   :   The Proof of Faith

YEAR 1

Psalm 56

Old Testament Jeremiah 7, 1-11

Epistle James 1, 16-27

8	Now that the daylight fills the sky
* 265	O Lord of heaven and earth and sea
* 308	We plough the fields, and scatter

Gospel Luke 17, 11-19

662	Jesus Christ is passing by
* 479	Now thank we all our God
* 481	Praise, my soul, the King of heaven
476	Fill thou my life, O Lord my God

YEAR 2

Psalm 57

Old Testament Jeremiah 32, 6-15

Epistle Galatians 2, 15- 3, 9

Gospel Luke 7, 1-10

* 225	I am not worthy, Holy Lord
616	Jesu, high in glory

126

General Choice

Theme   :   The Offering of Life

YEAR 1

Psalm

145, 14-21

| | 302 | Good is the Lord, our heavenly King |
| | * 147 | Lord, in thy Name thy servants plead |

Old Testament

Deuteronomy 26, 1-11

| | 298 | Fair waved the golden corn |

Epistle

2 Corinthians 8, 1-9

| | 269 | Lord, speak to me, that I may speak |
| | 38 † | Good is our God who made this place |

Gospel

Matthew 5, 17-26

| | 545 | O Lord, and Master of us all |
| | 540 | O brother man! Fold to thy heart thy brother |

YEAR 2

Psalm

90, 13-17

Old Testament

Nehemiah 6, 1-16

Ecclesiaticus   38, 24-34

Epistle

1 Peter 4, 7-11

	555	Teach me, my God and King
	287	From thee all skill and science flow
	563	O thou who camest from above
	* 669	Take my life, and let it be

Gospel

Matthew 25, 14-30

| | 551 | Son of God, eternal Saviour |

General Choice

THE NINETEENTH SUNDAY AFTER PENTECOST

Theme : The Life of Faith

YEAR 1

Psalm   139, 1-11

Old Testament Genesis 28, 10-22

454	Lo, God is here, let us adore
* 592	Nearer, my God, to thee
102 †	As Jacob with travel was weary one day
* 506	O God of Bethel, by whose hand

Epistle   Hebrews 11, 1-2 & 8-16

261	In our day of thanksgiving one psalm let us offer
* 191	For all the saints, who from their labours rest
190	For all thy saints, O Lord
514	We've no abiding city here

Gospel   Matthew 6, 24-34

546	O Lord, how happy should we be
547	Put thou thy trust in God

YEAR 2

Psalm   65, 1-7   (1-8)

Old Testament Daniel 6, 10-23

Epistle   Romans 5, 1-11

580	Jesu, grant me this I pray
* 392	There is a green hill far away
106	O Love divine! What hast thou done?
* 403	Come down, O Love divine

Gospel   Luke 19, 1-10

* 477	Ye servants of God, your Master proclaim
662	Jesus Christ is passing by

General Choice

THE TWENTIETH SUNDAY AFTER PENTECOST

Theme   :   Endurance

YEAR 1

Psalm   37, 35-41

Old Testament   Daniel 3, 13-26

Epistle   Romans 8, 18-25

                536   Light of the lonely pilgrim's heart
                543   O God of truth, whose living word

Gospel   Luke 9, 51-62

         * 575   Dear Lord and Father of mankind
         * 554   Take up thy cross, the Saviour said

YEAR 2

Psalm   121

         * 513   To Zion's hill I lift my eyes

Old Testament   Genesis 32, 22-30

                559   Come, O thou traveller unknown
                565   Shepherd divine, our wants relieve

Epistle   1 Corinthians 9, 19-27

         * 530   Fight the good fight with all thy might!

Gospel   Matthew 7, 13-27

                521   Believe not those who say
                563   O thou who camest from above

THE TWENTY-FIRST SUNDAY AFTER PENTECOST

Theme : The Christian Hope

YEAR 1

Psalm 126

Old Testament Habakkuk 2, 1-4

For the Epistle Acts 26, 1-8

Gospel Luke 18 1-8

        560   Lord, teach us how to pray aright
        58 † Lord Jesus Christ

YEAR 2

Psalm 11

Old Testament Ezekiel 12, 21-28

Epistle 1 Peter 1, 13-21

    * 493   Children of the heavenly King
      69 † Now is eternal life

Gospel John 11, 17-27

      69 † Now is eternal life
     144   Ye choirs of new Jerusalem

General Choice

	130	'Christ the Lord is risen today'
	270	Christ is the world's true Light
	281	Lord, her watch thy Church is keeping
	354	Praise the Lord! ye heavens adore him
	365	Give to our God immortal praise
*	373	In the Name of Jesus
	397	Rejoice, the Lord is King!
	418	Hail to the Lord's Anointed
	473	A safe stronghold our God is still
	492	All my hope on God is founded
*	504	O God, our help in ages past
	510	The Lord my pasture shall prepare
*	512	The King of love my Shepherd is
	514	We've no abiding city here
	547	Put thou thy trust in God
*	548	Soldiers of Christ, arise
*	556	Through the night of doubt and sorrow
	573	As pants the hart for cooling streams
	597	Jesu, the very thought of thee (Part 1)
	14 †	Christ, who knows all his sheep
	56 †	Lord God, thou art our maker and our end
	68 †	Not far beyond the sea, nor high
	95 †	Thine be the glory, risen, conquering Son
	102 †	As Jacob with travel was weary one day
	116 †	Come, let us with our Lord arise
	120 †	Faithful vigil ended

THE TWENTY-SECOND SUNDAY
AFTER PENTECOST

Theme : The Two Ways

Psalm   119, 1-8

                             112

Old Testament   Deuteronomy 11, 18-28

Epistle   1 John 2, 22-29

Gospel   Luke 16, 1-9

                                 551   Son of God, eternal Saviour

General Choice

THE LAST SUNDAY AFTER PENTECOST

Theme : Citizens of Heaven

YEAR 1

Psalm	15
Old Testament	Jeremiah 29, 1 & 4-14
Epistle	Philippians 3, 7-21

	444	Sing Hallelujah forth in duteous praise
*	439	Light's abode, celestial Salem

Gospel	John 17, 1-10

	69 †	Now is eternal life
	484	Sing praise to God who reigns above
	400	When morning gilds the skies

YEAR 2

Psalm	146
Old Testament	Isaiah 33, 17-22
For the Epistle	Revelation 7, 2-4 & 9-17

	189	Who are these like stars appearing
	194	How bright those glorious spirits shine!
*	192	Give me the wings of faith to rise
	378	Look, ye saints, the sight is glorious
*	489	Ye holy angels bright
*	331	Holy, Holy, Holy! Lord God Almighty

Gospel	Matthew 25, 1-13

	686	Sleepers wake! for night is flying
	557	Ye servants of the Lord

General Choice

* 191   For all the saints, who from their labours rest
* 328   Bright the vision that delighted
* 335   My God, how wonderful thou art
   362   Come, let us join our cheerful songs
* 391   Ten thousand times ten thousand
* 415   Glorious things of thee are spoken
   434   Jerusalem, my happy home
* 437   Jerusalem the golden
   438   Let saints on earth in concert sing
   441   O what the joy and the glory must be
   445   There is a land of pure delight
   449   Christ is our corner-stone
* 477   Ye servants of God, your Master proclaim
* 493   Children of the heavenly King
* 556   Through the night of doubt and sorrow
   557   Ye servants of the Lord
   578   For ever with the Lord
   102 †   As Jacob with travel was weary one day
   139 †   How shall I sing that majesty
   155 †   Lord God, we give you thanks for all your saints
   199 †   Ye watchers and ye holy ones

SECTION 2

HYMNS FOR SAINTS' DAYS AND HOLY DAYS

January 1	**THE NAMING OF JESUS** (formerly "THE CIRCUMCISION OF CHRIST")

Psalm	8

	198 †	With wonder, Lord , we see your works

62, 1-8

Old Testament	Isaiah 9, 2 & 6-7

	81	The people that in darkness sat
	C26	Unto us is born a Son

For the Epistle	Acts 4, 8-12

	71	Jesus! Name of wondrous love!
	399	To the name of our salvation
	361	Conquering kings their titles take
	259	Christ is made the sure foundation
	441	O what the joy and the glory must be

Gospel	Luke 2, 15-21

	55	Blessed night, when first that plain
	C 9	God rest you merry, gentlemen
*	C17	See amid the winter's snow
*	C29	When the crimson sun had set
	60	Love came down at Christmas

General Choice	*	359	All hail the power of Jesu's Name
	*	596	How sweet the Name of Jesus sounds
		598	There is a Name I love to hear

January 25	**THE CONVERSION OF SAINT PAUL**

Psalm	126

67

	*	417	God of mercy, God of grace

Old Testament	1 Kings 19, 15-21
For the Epistle	Acts 9, 1-22
	168 We sing the glorious conquest
Gospel	Matthew 19, 27-30
General Choice	197 Disposer supreme, and Judge of the earth
	* 421 Jesus shall reign where'er the sun
	9 † Awake, awake: fling off the night!

February 1	**SAINT BRIGID**
Psalm	134
Old Testament	Hosea 6, 1-4
Epistle	1 John 1, 1-4
	472 O Word of God incarnate
	* 284 Thou whose almighty word
Gospel	John 10, 7-16
	623 Loving shepherd of thy sheep
	670 Souls of men, why will ye scatter
General Choice	203 Lord, who in thy perfect wisdom

THE PRESENTATION OF CHRIST
IN THE TEMPLE

Psalm	48
	Nunc Dimittis
	120 † Faithful vigil ended
Old Testament	Malachi 3, 1-5
Epistle	1 Peter 2, 1-10
	449 Christ is our corner-stone
	* 596 How sweet the Name of Jesus sounds
	259 Christ is made the sure foundation
Gospel	Luke 2, 22-35
	169 In his temple now behold him
	* 590 Love Divine, all loves excelling
	120 † Faithul vigil ended
General Choice	211 Come, ever-blessed Spirit, come
	462 Sweet is the solemn voice that calls
	464 To thy temple I repair
	* 523 Blest are the pure in heart

March 17	# SAINT PATRICK
Psalm	145, 1-13
	346 All creatures of our God and King
	* 482 Praise to the Lord, the Almighty, the King of creation
Old Testament	Tobit 13, 1b-7
	Deuteronomy 32, 1-9
	316 Rejoice, O land, in God thy might
	317 To thee our God we fly (vv.1-3 & 9)
	18 † Creator of the earth and skies

Epistle	2 Corinthians 4, 1-12	
	171	Thus spake the risen Master
	278	Light of them that sit in darkness!
	197	Disposer supreme, and Judge of the earth
	* 284	Thou whose almighty word
Gospel	John 4, 31-38	
	268	Lord of the living harvest
General Choice	193	God, whose city's sure foundation
	203	Lord, who in thy perfect wisdom
	313	Lift thy banner, Church of Erin
	* 326	I bind unto myself today
	183 †	This day God gives me

March 25 **THE ANNUNCIATION OF OUR LORD TO THE BLESSED VIRGIN MARY**

Psalm	113	
	131	
Old Testament	Isaiah 52, 7-10	
Epistle	Galatians 4, 1-5	
	491	Behold the amazing gift of love
Gospel	Luke 1, 26-38a	
	172	Praise we the Lord this day
	89 †	Tell out, my soul, the greatness of the Lord
	86 †	Sing we a song of high revolt
	27 †	For Mary, Mother of our Lord
General Choice	58	From east to west, from shore to shore
	67	Of the Father's love begotten (omit v.3)

145

SAINT MARK

Psalm   45, 1-5   (1-6)

                              119, 9-16

Old Testament   Proverbs 15, 28-33

Epistle   Ephesians 4, 7-16

                              155   The Lord ascendeth up on high
                              257   O thou who makest souls to shine
                              401   Where high the heavenly temple stand*

Gospel   Mark 13, 5-13

                              521   Believe not those who say
                            * 322   Be thou my vision, O Lord of my he.

General Choice   173   We praise your grace, O Saviour
                            * 470   Lord, thy word abideth
                              1 †   A Man there lived in Galilee

May 1   SAINT PHILIP AND SAINT JAMES

Psalm   33, 1-5

                              25, 1-10   (1-9)

Old Testament   Proverbs 4, 10-18

Epistle   Ephesians 1, 3-14

                              502   May the grace of Christ our Saviour
                              23 †   Father, Lord of all Creation

Gospel   John 14, 1-14

	395	Thou art the Way: to thee alone
*	553	Thine for ever! God of love
	564	Prayer is the soul's sincere desire
	524	Brothers, joining hand to hand
	251	We pray thee, heavenly Father
	79 †	O Lord, we long to see your face
	107 †	Christ is the world's light, he and none other

General Choice   270   Christ is the world's true Light
                      543   O God of truth, whose living word

May 14   SAINT MATTHIAS

Psalm   16. 1-6   (1-7)

                    80. 8-15

Old Testament   1 Samuel 2, 27-35

For the Epistle Acts 1, 15-17 & 20-26
                      170   The highest and the holiest place

Gospel   John 15, 1-11

	502	May the grace of Christ our Saviour
*	590	Love Divine, all loves excelling
*	415	Glorious things of thee are spoken

General Choice   196   Captains of the saintly band
                      198   The eternal gifts of Christ the King

147

May 31	THE VISITATION OF THE BLESSED VIRGIN MARY	

Psalm	113	
	131	
Old Testament	Zechariah 2, 10-13	
	286	Zion's King shall reign victorious
Epistle	Galatians 4, 1-5	
	491	Behold the amazing gift of love
Gospel	Luke 1, 39-49	
	89 †	Tell out, my soul, the greatness of the Lord
	86 †	Sing we a song of high revolt

June 9	SAINT COLUMBA	

Psalm	34, 9-15	
	* 485	Through all the changing scenes of life
Old Testament	Micah 4, 1-5	
	270	Christ is the world's true Light
Epistle	Romans 15, 1-6	
	518	Help us to help each other, Lord
	47 †	Jesus, Lord, we look to thee
	468	God hath spoken - by his prophets
Gospel	John 12, 20-26	
General Choice	202	In the roll-call of God's sons
	203	Lord, who in thy perfect wisdom

SAINT BARNABAS

Psalm   145, 8-15

                                346   All creatures of our God and King
                            * 482   Praise to the Lord, the Almighty,
                                                the King of creation

                     112

Old Testament   Job 29, 11-16

For the Epistle   Acts 11, 19-30

                                174   O Son of God, our Captain of salvation

Gospel   John 15, 12-17

                                515   Beloved, let us love: love is of God
                                518   Help us to help each other, Lord

General Choice   277   In Christ there is no east or west
                            * 403   Come down, O Love divine
                                540   O brother man!   Fold to thy heart thy
                                                brother

June 24   **THE BIRTH OF SAINT JOHN THE BAPTIST**

Psalm   80. 1-7

                     119, 161-168

                                478   King of glory, King of peace

Old Testament   Isaiah 40, 1-11

                            *   51   On Jordan's bank the Baptist's cry
                                51 †   Lo, in the wilderness a voice

For the Epistle   Acts 13, 16-26

Gospel   Luke 1, 57-66 & 80

                                175   The great forerunner of the morn

General Choice   *   43   Come, thou long-expected Jesus
                            *   44   Hark! a thrilling voice is sounding
                            *   45   Hark the glad sound! the Saviour comes

Psalm	125 *or* 18, 33-37 (32-36)
Old Testament	Ezekiel 3, 4-11
Epistle	1 Peter 2, 19-25

           537   Lord, as to thy dear Cross we flee
           505   O happy band of pilgrims
            1 †   A Man there lived in Galilee

Gospel	Matthew 16, 13-20

           176   Thou art the Christ, O Lord
        * 554   Take up thy cross, the Saviour said

General Choice	

           196   Captains of the saintly band
           198   The eternal gifts of Christ the King
           423   Lord of our life, and God of our salvatic
           449   Christ is our corner-stone

July 3   SAINT THOMAS

Psalm	139, 1-11
Old Testament	Genesis 12, 1-4

           332   The God of Abraham praise
        * 506   O God of Bethel, by whose hand

Epistle	Hebrews 10, 35- 11, 1

           521   Believe not those who say

Gospel	John 20, 24-29

           167   O thou who didst with love untold
           136   O sons and daughters, let us sing!
        * 453   Jesu, stand among us
           586   Jesus, these eyes have never seen

Psalm	15	
	75, 6-11 (7-12)	
Old Testament	Jeremiah 45	
For the Epistle	Acts 11, 27- 12, 2	
	177	For all thy saints, a noble throng
Gospel	Mark 10, 35-45	
	132 †	God is love, and where true love is, God himself is there
	97 †	We find thee, Lord, in other's need
	195 †	Where love and loving-kindness dwell
General Choice	196	Captains of the saintly band

August 6   THE TRANSFIGURATION OF OUR LORD

Psalm	84	
	456	How lovely are thy dwellings fair!
	459	Pleasant are thy courts above
	166 †	Now from the altar of our hearts
Old Testament	Exodus 34, 29-35	

Epistle	2 Corinthians 3, 4-18		
		* 453	Jesu, stand among us
		* 590	Love Divine, all loves excelling
Gospel	Luke 9, 28-36		
		179	'Tis good, Lord, to be here!
		178	Upon the holy Mount they stood
		108 †	Christ upon the mountain peak
		169 †	O raise you eyes on high and see
General Choice		* 3	Christ, whose glory fills the skies
		215	Author of life divine
		270	Christ is the world's true Light
		* 322	Be thou my vision, O Lord of my heart
		* 335	My God, how wonderful thou art
		452	God reveals his presence
		486	When all thy mercies, O my God
		565	Shepherd divine, our wants relieve
		586	Jesus, these eyes have never seen
		597	Jesu, the very thought of thee (Part 1)
		597	O Jesu, King most wonderful (Part 2)

August 24	**SAINT BARTHOLOMEW**		
Psalm	116, 11-18 (11-16)		
	97		
		340	The Lord is King! Lift up thy voice
Old Testament	Isaiah 61, 4-9		
For the Epistle	Acts 5, 12 ·16		
		288	O God, whose will is life and good
Gospel	Luke 22, 24-30		
		195 †	Where love and loving-kindness dwell
General Choice		180	King of saints, to whom the number

153

Psalm	45, 10-17 (11-18)	
	Magnificat	
	89 †	Tell out, my soul, the greatness of the Lord
	86 †	Sing we a song of high revolt
Old Testament	Micah 5, 2-4	
For the Epistle	Revelation 21, 1-7	
	441	O what the joy and the glory must be
	* 439	Light's abode, celestial Salem
	343	Songs of praise the angels sang
	* 590	Love Divine, all loves excelling
Gospel	Luke 1, 39-49	
	89 †	Tell out, my soul, the greatness of the Lord
	86 †	Sing we a song of high revolt
	27 †	For Mary, Mother of our Lord
	Luke 2, 1-19	
	C 3	A Virgin most pure, as the prophet foretold
	* 68	While shepherds watched their flocks by night
	* C17	See amid the winter's snow
	* C21	Still the night, holy the night!
	C12	I know a rose-tree springing

September 21	**SAINT MATTHEW**	
Psalm	119, 65-72 *or* 119, 89-96	
Old Testament	Proverbs 3, 9-18	
	298	Fair waved the golden corn
Epistle	2 Corinthians 4, 1-6	
	278	Light of them that sit in darkness!
	197	Disposer supreme, and Judge of the earth
	* 284	Thou whose almighty word
Gospel	Matthew 9, 9-13	
	181	He sat to watch o'er customs paid
	* 575	Dear Lord and Father of mankind

General Choice		
	* 322	Be thou my vision, O Lord of my heart
	551	Son of God, eternal Saviour

September 29   SAINT MICHAEL AND ALL ANGELS

Psalm		
	103, 17-22	
	* 489	Ye holy angels bright
	91, 5-12	

Old Testament		
	2 Kings 6, 8-17	

For the Epistle		
	Revelation 12, 7-12	
	184	Stars of the morning, so gloriously bright

Gospel		
	Matthew 18, 1-6 & 10	
	622	Lord Jesus, from thy throne above
	633	Through the night thy angels kept

General Choice		
	* 182	Hark, hark, my soul! angelic songs are swelling
	183	Around the throne of God a band
	185	They come, God's messengers of love
	343	Songs of praise the angels sang
	354	Praise the Lord! ye heavens adore him
	362	Come, let us join our cheerful songs
	* 474	Angel voices, ever singing
	480	O praise ye the Lord! Praise him in the height
	* 481	Praise, my soul, the King of heaven
	* 489	Ye holy angels bright
	199 †	Ye watchers and ye holy ones

Psalm	147, 1-6
	22, 23-29 (22-28)
Old Testament	Isaiah 35, 3-6
For the Epistle	Acts 16, 6-12a

278	Light of them that sit in darkness!
* 322	Be thou my vision, O Lord of my heart

Epistle	2 Timothy 4, 5-13

186	What thanks and praise to thee we owe

Gospel	Luke 10, 1-9

268	Lord of the living harvest
281	Lord, her watch thy Church is keeping
* 477	Ye servants of God, your Master proclaim

General Choice

20	At even, when the sun did set
287	From thee all skill and science flow
288	O God, whose will is life and good
289	Thine arm, O Lord, in days of old
290	Thou to whom the sick and dying
87 †	Son of the Lord Most High

Psalm   15

                        116, 11-18   (11-16)

Old Testament   Isaiah 28, 9-16

                        259   Christ is made the sure foundation

Epistle   Ephesians 2, 13-22

                        277   In Christ there is no east or west
                        106 †   Christ is the heavenly food that gives
                        449   Christ is our corner-stone

Gospel   John 14, 15-26

                        * 403   Come down, O Love divine
                        * 161   Our blest Redeemer, ere he breathed

General Choice   449   Christ is our corner-stone
                                7 †   As the bridegroom to his chosen

Psalm	145, 8-13	
	346	All creatures of our God and King
	* 482	Praise to the Lord, the Almighty, the King of creation
Old Testament	Jeremiah 31, 31-34	
	541	O for a heart to praise my God
	2 Esdras 2, 42-48	
For the Epistle	Revelation 7, 2-4 & 9-17	
	189	Who are these like stars appearing
	194	How bright those glorious spirits shine!
	* 192	Give me the wings of faith to rise
	378	Look, ye saints, the sight is glorious
	* 489	Ye holy angels bright
Epistle	Hebrews 12, 18-24	
	* 415	Glorious things of thee are spoken
	434	Jerusalem, my happy home
	* 513	To Zion's hill I lift my eyes
Gospel	Matthew 5, 1-12	
	* 523	Blest are the pure in heart
	Luke 6, 20-23	
	* 523	Blest are the pure in heart
General Choice	187	The saints of God! their conflict past
	188	For thy saints unknown to fame
	190	For all thy saints, O Lord
	* 191	For all the saints, who from their labours rest
	204	For those we love within the veil
	205	O God, to whom the faithful dead
	206	God of the living, in whose eyes
	261	In our day of thanksgiving one psalm let us off
	* 331	Holy, Holy, Holy! Lord God Almighty
	* 384	The head that once was crowned with thorns
	* 391	Ten thousand times ten thousand
	* 430	The Church's one foundation
	* 431	Thy hand, O God, has guided

158

General Choice	434	Jerusalem, my happy home
(continued)	436	He wants not friends that hath thy love
	* 437	Jerusalem, the golden
	* 439	Light's abode, celestial Salem
	441	O what the joy and the glory must be
	445	There is a land of pure delight
	* 504	O God, our help in ages past
	30 †	Glory to thee, O God
	139 †	How shall I sing that majesty
	155 †	Lord God, we give you thanks for all your saints
	175 †	Rejoice in God's saints, today and all days
	199 †	Ye watchers and ye holy ones

November 30   SAINT ANDREW

Psalm   92, 1-5

	37	Sweet is the work, my God, my King
87		
	* 415	Glorious things of thee are spoken

Old Testament   Zechariah 8, 20-23

Epistle   Romans 10, 12-18

	281	Lord, her watch thy Church is keeping

Gospel   Matthew 4, 12-20

	* 166	Jesus calls us! o'er the tumult
	283	O Master! when thou callest
	49 †	Jesus our Lord, our King and our God

General Choice

	270	Christ is the world's true light
	273	'For my sake and the gospel's, go'
	277	In Christ there is no east or west
	282	Spread, O spread, thou mighty word
	* 284	Thou whose almighty word
	137 †	Hills of the North, rejoice

159

SAINT STEPHEN

Psalm	119, 17-24
	119, 161-168
	478 King of glory, King of peace
Old Testament	2 Chronicles 24, 20-22
For the Epistle	Acts 7, 54-60
	340 The Lord is King! lift up thy voice
	195 The Son of God goes forth to war
Gospel	Matthew 23, 34-39
General Choice	* 359 All hail the power of Jesu's Name

SAINT JOHN THE EVANGELIST

Psalm	117
	337 From all that dwell below the skies
	92, 12-15
Old Testament	Exodus 33, 12-23
Epistle	1 John 2, 1-11
	515 Beloved, let us love: love is of God
	518 Help us to help each other, Lord
Gospel	John 21, 20-25
	69 Word supreme, before creation

General Choice	* 229	Jesu, thou Joy of loving hearts
	491	Behold the amazing gift of love
	* 590	Love Divine, all loves excelling
	* 596	How sweet the Name of Jesus sounds
	683	Jesu, priceless treasure

December 28   **THE HOLY INNOCENTS**

Psalm   123

           131

Old Testament   Jeremiah 31, 15-17

Epistle   1 Corinthians 1, 26-29

Gospel   Matthew 2, 13-18

| | 70 | When Christ was born in Bethlehem |
| | C26 | Unto us is born a Son |

General Choice	* 493	Children of the heavenly King
	* 620	Jesus loves me: this I know
	621	Jesus, tender Shepherd, hear me
	* 626	Saviour, like a shepherd, lead us
	628	There's a friend for little children

SECTION 3

HYMNS FOR SPECIAL OCCASIONS

Psalm

122

84, 8-13

166 †   Now from the altar of our hearts

Old Testament

Jeremiah 1, 4-10

Numbers 11, 16-17 & 24-29

Numbers 27, 15-23

Epistle

1 Peter 4, 7-11

555   Teach me, my God and King
257   O thou who makest souls to shine
563   O thou who camest from above
* 669   Take my life, and let it be

For the Epistle

Acts 20, 28-35

* 429   Thy kingdom come, O God
258.   Pour out thy Spirit from on high

Epistle

1 Corinthians 3, 3-11

449   Christ is our corner-stone

Gospel

Luke 12, 35-43

557   Ye servants of the Lord

Luke 4, 16-21

* 45   Hark .the glad sound! the Saviour comes
467   Father of mercies, in thy word

John 4, 31-38

268   Lord of the living harvest
281   Lord, her watch thy Church is keeping
282   Spread, O spread, thou mighty word

THANKSGIVING FOR HARVEST

Psalm	65	
	67	
	* 417	God of mercy, God of grace
	104, 21-30	(19-28)
	* 352	O worship the King all-glorious above
	302	Good is the Lord, our heavenly King
	145	
	346	All creatures of our God and King
	* 482	Praise to the Lord, the Almighty, the King of creation
	302	Good is the Lord, our heavenly King
	* 147	Lord, in thy Name thy servants plead
Old Testament	Genesis 1, 1-3 & 24-31a	
	* 602	All things bright and beautiful
	* 284	Thou whose almighty word
	346	All creatures of our God and King
	* 349	I sing the almighty power of God
	351	Lord of beauty, thine the splendour
	356	The spacious firmament on high
	Deuteronomy 8, 1-10	
	316	Rejoice, O land, in God thy might
	Deuteronomy 26, 1-11	
	298	Fair waved the golden corn
	Deuteronomy 28, 1-14	
For the Epistle	Acts 10, 10-16	
	Acts 14, 13-17	
	265	O Lord of heaven and earth and sea
	* 353	Praise, O praise, our God and King
Epistle	2 Corinthians 9, 6-15	
	* 308	We plough the fields, and scatter
	1 Timothy 6, 6-10	
For the Epistle	Revelation 14, 14-18	
	268	Lord of the living harvest
Gospel	Matthew 6, 24-34	
	546	O Lord, how happy should we be
	547	Put thou thy trust in God

Gospel

Matthew 13, 18-30

447   Almighty God, thy word is cast
176 † Rise and hear! The Lord is speaking

Luke 12, 16-31

546   O Lord, how happy should we be
547   Put thou thy trust in God

John 4, 31-38

281   Lord, her watch thy Church is keeping

John 6, 27-35

106 † Christ is the heavenly food that gives
217   Bread of heaven, on thee we feed
* 219   Bread of the world, in mercy broken
227   I hunger and I thirst
* 229   Jesus, thou Joy of loving hearts
* 236   O God, unseen, yet ever near
144 † Jesus, we thus obey

General Choice

Any of the hymns in the Thanksgiving for Harvest Section (297-308), the Creator Section (345-357), or the following :-

* 132   Hallelujah! Hallelujah!
* 249   Upon thy table, Lord, we place
337   From all that dwell below the skies
* 344   Immortal, invisible, God only wise
* 479   Now thank we all our God
* 602   All things bright and beautiful
611   God, who made the earth
635   We thank thee, O our Father
38 † Good is our God who made this place
60 † Lord of all good, our gifts we bring to thee
82 † Praise and thanksgiving
124 † For the fruits of his creation
153 † Lord, by whose breath all souls and seeds are living
167 † Now join we, to praise the Creator
168 † Now the green blade riseth from the buried grain
174 † Reap me the earth as a harvest to God
177 † Sent forth by God's blessing, our true faith confessing

THE DEDICATION FESTIVAL OF A CHURCH

Psalm	84, 1-7	
	456	How lovely are thy dwellings fair!
	459	Pleasant are thy courts above
	122	

Old Testament	1 Kings 8, 22-30

Epistle	1 Peter 2, 1-10	
	259	Christ is made the sure foundation
	449	Christ is our corner-stone

Gospel	Matthew 21, 12-16	
	* 465	We love the place, O God
	461	Spirit divine, attend our prayer

General Choice	260	Only-begotten, Word of God eternal
	261	In our day of thanksgiving one psalm let us offer
	262	Our Father, by whose servants
	* 455	Great Shepherd of thy people, hear
	457	Jesus, where'er thy people meet
	462	Sweet is the solemn voice that calls
	463	Thou God of power and God of love
	464	To thy temple I repair
	* 474	Angel voices, ever singing
	478	King of glory, King of peace
	* 479	Now thank we all our God
	480	O praise ye the Lord! Praise him in the height
	112 †	Christians, lift up your hearts, and make this a day of rejoicing
	131 †	God is here; as we his people

COMMUNITY AND WORLD PEACE

Psalm	72, 1-7	
	85. 8-13	
Old Testament	Micah 4, 1-5	
	270	Christ is the world's true Light
Epistle	1 Timothy 2, 1-6	
	28 †	For the healing of the nations
	99 †	What does the Lord require
Gospel	Matthew 5, 43-48	
	524	Brothers, joining hand to hand
	518	Help us to help each other, Lord
General Choice	277	In Christ there is no east or west
	* 315	Lord, while for all mankind we pray
	317	To thee our God we fly (vv.1-3 & 8-9)
	318	God the all-terrible; King who ordainest
	319	O God of love, O King of peace
	410	Almighty Father, who dost give
	* 429	Thy kingdom come, O God
	528	Eternal Ruler of the ceaseless round
	551	Son of God, eternal Saviour
	18 †	Creator of the earth and skies
	22 †	Father all-powerful, thine is the kingdom
	44 †	In humble gratitude, O God
	63 †	Lord of lords and King eternal
	64 †	Lord, save the world; in bitter need
	72 †	O Day of God, draw nigh
	92 †	The God who rules this earth
	107 †	Christ is the wold's light, he and none other
	137 †	Hills of the North, rejoice
	167 †	Now join we, to praise the Creator
	181 †	There in God's garden stands the tree of wisd
	189 †	We turn to you, O God of every nation

THE UNITY OF THE CHURCH

Psalm	133
	122
Old Testament	Jeremiah 33, 6-9
Epistle	Ephesians 4, 1-6

	431	Thy hand, O God, has guided
	132 †	God is love, and where true love is,
		God himself is there

Gospel John 17, 11b-23

*	241	O thou who at thy Eucharist didst pray
	422	Jesus, thou hast willed it
	53 †	Lord Christ, the Father's mighty Son
	551	Son of God, eternal Saviour

General Choice

	223	Father, we thank thee who hast planted
	277	In Christ there is no east or west
*	411	City of God, how broad and far
	426	Put forth, O God, thy Spirit's might
*	430	The Church's one foundation
	524	Brothers, joining hand to hand
	528	Eternal Ruler of the ceaseless round
*	556	Through the night of doubt and sorrow
	12 †	Christ is the King! O friends rejoice
	26 †	Filled with the Spirit's power, with one accord
	47 †	Jesus, Lord, we look to thee
	53 †	Lord Christ, the Father's mighty Son
	63 †	Lord of lords and King eternal
	92 †	The God who rules this earth
	106 †	Christ is the heavenly food that gives
	107 †	Christ is the world's light, he and none other
	140 †	I come with joy to meet my Lord
	141 †	In Adam we have all been one
	148 †	Let us talents and tongues employ
	162 †	Lord, to you we bring our treasure
	195 †	Where love and loving-kindness dwell

THE GUIDANCE OF THE HOLY SPIRIT
SUITABLE AT THE OPENING OF MEETINGS OF
SYNOD OR VESTRY

Psalm   25, 1-10   (1-9)
                     143, 8-10

Old Testament   Isaiah 30, 15-21
                     Wisdom 9, 13-17

Epistle   1 Corinthians 12, 4-13
                         157   Come, thou Holy Spirit, come

                     Philippians 2, 1-11
                       * 373   In the Name of Jesus
                          4 †   All praise to thee, for thou, O King divine
                       * 523   Blest are the pure in heart

Gospel   John 14, 23-26
                       * 403   Come down, O Love divine

                     John 16, 13-15
                       * 405   Come, gracious Spirit, heavenly Dove

General Choice   * 156   Come, Holy Ghost, our souls inspire
                         158   Creator Spirit, by whose aid
                         160   O Holy Ghost, thy people bless
                         162   Spirit of mercy, truth and love
                         406   Holy Spirit, truth divine
                         528   Eternal Ruler of the ceaseless round
                          26 † Filled with the Spirit's power, with one accord
                         138 † Holy Spirit, come, confirm us
                         145 † Let every Christian pray
                         171 † On the day of Pentecost
                         182 † There's a spirit in the air
                         193 † When Jesus came to Jordan

THE SPREAD OF THE GOSPEL

Psalm	97	
	340	The Lord is King! lift up thy voice
	100	
	* 333	All people that on earth do dwell
	334	Before Jehovah's aweful throne
Old Testament	Isaiah 49, 1-6	
Epistle	Ephesians 2, 13-22	
	277	In Christ there is no east or west
	106 †	Christ is the heavenly food that gives
	449	Christ is our corner-stone
	259	Christ is made the sure foundation
Gospel	Matthew 28, 16-20	
	273	'For my sake and the gospel's, go'
	409	O Spirit of the living God
	282	Spread, O spread, thou mighty word
	* 477	Ye servants of God, your Master proclaim
General Choice		Any of the Hymns in the Church Overseas
		Section (270-286), or any of the following :-
	414	O Lord our God, arise!
	* 417	God of mercy, God of grace
	* 421	Jesus shall reign where'er the sun
	428	Rise up, O men of God
	447	Almighty God, thy word is cast
	11 †	Christ for the world we sing
	22(i)†	Father all-powerful, thine is the kingdom
	22(ii)†	Father all-loving, thou rulest in majesty
	63 †	Lord of lords and King eternal
	109 †	Christ, when for us you were baptized
	125 †	Forth in the peace of Christ we go
	145 †	Let every Christian pray
	148 †	Let us talents and tongues employ
	186 †	We are your people
	196 †	Who are we who stand and sing?

THE APPOINTMENT OF A BISHOP OR AN INCUMBENT

Psalm	15
	25, 1-6 (1-5)
Old Testament	Numbers 11, 16-17 & 24-29
	1 Samuel 16, 1-13a
For the Epistle	Acts 1, 15-17 & 20-26
	170 The highest and the holiest place
Epistle	Ephesians 4, 7-16
	155 The Lord ascendeth up on high
	257 O thou who makest souls to shine
	401 Where high the heavenly temple stands
Gospel	John 4, 34-38
	268 Lord of the living harvest
	John 15, 9-17
	515 Beloved, let us love: love is of God
	518 Help us to help each other, Lord

A PARTICULAR COMMEMORATION

Readings may be selected as appropriate from the provisions of ALL SAINTS (page 158) or from the following:

Psalm	32
	34, 1-10 *or* 34, 11-18
	* 485 Through all the changing scenes of life
	114 † Christians, lift your hearts and voices
	112
	119, 1-8
Old Testament	Proverbs 8, 1-11
	Proverbs 31, 10-31
	Malachi 2, 5-7
	Ecclesiasticus 2, 1-6
	521 Believe not those who say
	520 Awake our souls! away our fears!
Epistle	2 Corinthians 4, 11-18
	* 439 Light's abode, celestial Salem
	Hebrews 13, 1-3
	518 Help us to help each other, Lord
	519 O praise our God today
	100 † When I needed a neighbour, were you there?
	515 Beloved, let us love: love is of God
	Ephesians 4, 22-32
	9† Awake, awake: fling off the night!
	Ephesians 6, 11-18
	* 548 Soldiers of Christ, arise
	549 Soldiers of the Cross, arise!
	* 552 Stand up, stand up for Jesus
	507 Oft in danger, oft in woe
	526 Christian, ssek no yet repose

Gospel

Matthew 19, 16-21

    551   Son of God, eternal Saviour

Matthew 25, 31-46

    100 †   When I needed a neighbour, were you there?
    675   Thou didst leave thy throne and thy kingly
               crown

Mark 10, 42-45

    132 †   God is love, and where true love is,
               God himself is there
    97 †   We find thee, Lord, in others' need
    195 †   Where love and loving-kindness dwell

Luke 10, 38-42

    386   O Love, who formedst me to wear

MOTHERING SUNDAY

Psalm	27, 1-6	
	34	
	* 485	Through all the changing scenes of life
	114 †	Christians, lift your hearts and voices
	566	There is an eye that never sleeps
	84	
	456	How lovely are thy dwellings fair!
	459	Pleasant are thy courts above
	166 †	Now from the altar of our hearts
	87	
	* 415	Glorious things of thee are spoken
	122	
	139, 1-18	
Old Testament	1 Samuel 1, 20-28	
	Proverbs 4, 1-9	
	Proverbs 31, 10-31	
	Micah 4, 1-5	
	270	Christ is the world's true Light
Epistle	Colossians 3, 12-17	
	343	Songs of praise the angels sang
	555	Teach me, my God and King
	47 †	Jesus, Lord, we look to thee
	* 474	Angel voices, ever singing
	* 479	Now thank we all our God
	2 Timothy 1, 3-10	
	182 †	There's a spirit in the air
	282	Spread, O spread, thou mighty word
	1 Peter 2, 1-10	
	259	Christ is made the sure foundation
	449	Christ is our corner-stone

Gospel   Mark 10, 13-16

291	Our Father, by whose name
619	Jesus, Friend of little children
631	Thou who once on mother's knee

Luke 2, 41-52

80	The heavenly Child in stature grows
* 612	I love to hear the story
619	Jesus, Friend of little children

John 19, 23-27

571	When our heads are bowed with woe
* 109	O scared head, surrounded

General Choice

* 345	For the beauty of the earth
* 577	Hark, my soul! it is the Lord

REMEMBRANCE SUNDAY

Psalm	46	
	473	A safe stronghold our God is still
	47	
	93	
	126	
	130	

Old Testament	Isaiah 2, 1-5	
	270	Christ is the world's true Light
	432	Thy kingdom come! on bended knee
	Isaiah 10, 33- 11, 9	
	* 274	God is working his purpose out as year succeeds to year
	Ezekiel 37, 1-14	
	* 402	Breathe on me, Breath of God
	409	O Spirit of the living God

Epistle	Romans 8, 31-39	
	* 364	Crown him with many crowns (vv. 1, 3, 4-6)
	568	Jesus, thy Blood and righteousness
or the Epistle	Revelation 21, 1-7	
	76 †	O Holy City, seen of John
	441	O what the joy and the glory must be
	* 439	Light's abode, celestial Salem
	343	Songs of praise the angels sang
	* 590	Love Divine, all loves excelling

or the provisions for   Pentecost 14

Gospel

Matthew 5, 1-12

   * 523   Blest are the pure in heart

John 15, 9-17

   515   Beloved, let us love; love is of God
   518   Help us to help each other, Lord

General Choice

190	For all thy saints, O Lord
* 191	For all the saints, who from their labours rest
309	God of our fathers, known of old
311	God of our fathers, whose almighty hand
312	I vow to thee, my country, all earthly things abov
* 315	Lord, while for all mankind we pray
316	Rejoice, O land, in God thy might
317	To thee our God we fly (vv. 1-3 & 8-9)
318	God the all-terrible; King, who ordainest
319	O God of love, O King of peace
* 429	Thy kingdom come, O God
* 431	Thy hand, O God, has guided
441	O what the joy and the glory must be
* 504	O God, our help in ages past
528	Eternal Ruler of the ceaseless round
551	Son of God, eternal Saviour
5 †	Almighty Father, who for us thy Son didst give
18 †	Creator of the earth and skies
22(ii)†	Father all-loving, thou rulest in majesty
28 †	For the healing of the nations
35 †	God of love and truth and beauty
63 †	Lord of lords and King eternal
72 †	O Day of God, draw nigh
189 †	We turn to you, O God of every nation

LECTIONARY INDEX

The number following each lection indicates the page on which the reading is to be found

PROPER PSALMS

READINGS APPOINTED FOR THE OLD TESTAMENT LESSON

182

MICAH
4,1-5..... 116.148.168.175
5,2-4 ..... 28. 154
6,1-8 104
7,7-20 74

HABAKKUK
2,1-4 134

ZEPHANIAH
3,14-20 ..... 50. 151

ZECHARIAH
2,10-13 ..... 26. 148
8,20-23 159
9,9-12 66

MALACHI
2,5-7 173
3,1-5 ..... 24. 144

2 ESDRAS
2, 42-48 158

TOBIT
13,1b-7 144

WISDOM
9,13-17 170

ECCLESIASTICUS
2,1-6 173
3,2-7 32
38,24-34 128
42,15-25 44

READINGS APPOINTED FOR THE EPISTLE

ACTS
1,1-11 89
1,15-17 & 20-26 ..... 147.172
2,1-11 92
2,37-47 97
4,8-12 ..... 99. 142
5,12-16 153
7,54-60 160
7,54-8,1 118
8,26-38 101
9,1-22 143
10,10-16 165
10,34-38a 36
11,4-18 103
11,19-30 149
11,27-12,2 152
13,16-26 149
14,13-17 165
16,6-12a 156
17, 22-34 116
20, 17-35 118

ACTS (continued)
20,28-35 164
26,1-8 134
26,1 & 9-20 38

ROMANS
1,18-25 46
4,13-25 14
5,1-11 130
6,3-11 98
7,7-13 12
8,1-11 106
8,11-17 32
8,18-25 132
8,28-39 86
8,31-39 177
9,19-28 18
10,12-18 159
11,13-24 18
12,1-8 31

READINGS APPOINTED FOR THE GOSPEL

THEMATIC INDEX

The number following each theme indicates the page on which the subject is to be found.

SUNDAYS AND PRINCIPAL HOLY DAYS

SAINTS' DAYS AND HOLY DAYS

SPECIAL   OCCASIONS

HYMNS WHICH APPEAR IN BOTH THE
IRISH CHURCH HYMNAL AND HYMNS FOR TODAY

Hymns which have the same tune are marked with an asterisk

Irish Church Hymnal	Hundred Hymns for Today	TITLE OF HYMN
492	3	All my hope on God is founded
* 322	10	Be thou my vision, O Lord of my heart
270	13	Christ is the world's true light
220	16	Come, risen Lord, and deign to be our guest
* 528	20	Eternal Ruler of the ceaseless round
* 223	24	Father, we thank thee who hast planted
365	127	Give to our God immortal praise
341	32	God is Love : let heaven adore him
301	37	God, whose farm is all creation
* 518	41	Help us to help each other, Lord
* 276	137	Hills of the North, rejoice
277	43	In Christ there is no east or west
* 585	45	Jesus, good above all other
413	150	Lift up your heads, ye mighty gates
105	164	Nature with open volume stands
* 107	71	O crucified Redeemer
288	75	O God, whose will is life and good
* 291	172 †	Our Father, by whose Name
428	85	Rise up, O men of God
* 243	88	Strengthen for service, Lord, the hands
* 511	93	The Lord's my Shepherd, I'll not want
249	96	Upon thy table, Lord, we place
* 165	187	We give immortal praise

† *The form of addressing God in this hymn has been modernised in "Hymns for Today". This has led to a slight alteration in the word*